THE LIMITS OF FAITH

✡ ✝ ☪

The Limits of Faith

SEMA INSTITUTE

P.O.Box 570459
Miami, Florida, 33257
(305) 378-6253 Fax: (305) 378-6253

First U.S. edition © 2006 By Reginald Muata Ashby

All rights reserved. No part of this book may be used or reproduced in any manner whatsoever without written permission (address above) except in the case of brief quotations embodied in critical articles and reviews. All inquiries may be addressed to the address above.

The author is available for group lectures and individual counseling. For further information contact the publisher.

Ashby, Reginald Muata
The Limits of Faith: The Failure of Faith-based religion and the Solution to the Question of the Meaning of Life
 ISBN: 1-884564-62-3 (Hardcover), **ISBN**: 1-884564-63-1 (Softcover)

Library of Congress Cataloging in Publication Data

FOR MORE BOOKS BY THE AUTHOR
see back section of this volume

To order check at your local bookstore or Go to
http://www.booksurge.com/author.php3?accountID=LBGT00002

or call (305) 378-6253

The Limits of Faith
ABOUT THE AUTHOR

Mr. Ashby began studies in the area of religion and philosophy and achieved doctorates in these areas while at the same time he began to collect his research into what would later become several books on the subject of the African History, religion and ethics, world mythology, origins of Yoga Philosophy and practice in ancient Africa (Ancient Egypt/Nubia) and also the origins of Christian Mysticism in Ancient Egypt. He has extensively studied mystical religious traditions from around the world and is an accomplished lecturer, musician, artist, poet, painter, screenwriter, playwright and author of over 25 books on yoga philosophy, religious philosophy and social philosophy based on ancient African principles. A leading advocate of the concept of the existence of advanced social and religious philosophy in ancient Africa comparable to the Eastern traditions such as Vedanta, Buddhism, Confucianism and Taoism, he has lectured and written extensively on the correlations of these with ancient African religion and philosophy.

Muata Abhaya Ashby holds a Doctor of Philosophy Degree in Religion, and a Doctor of Divinity Degree in Holistic Health and a Masters Degree in Liberal Arts and Religious Studies. He is also a Pastoral Counselor and Teacher of Yoga Philosophy and Discipline. Dr. Ashby received his Doctor of Divinity Degree from and is an adjunct faculty member of Florida International university and the American Institute of Holistic Theology. Dr. Ashby is a certified as a PREP Relationship Counselor. Dr. Ashby has been an independent researcher and practitioner of Egyptian Yoga, Indian Yoga, Chinese Yoga, Buddhism and mystical psychology as well as Christian Mysticism. Dr. Ashby has engaged in Post Graduate research in advanced Jnana, Bhakti and Kundalini Yogas at the Yoga Research Foundation.

Dr. Ashby began his research into the spiritual philosophy of Ancient Egypt and India and noticed correlations in the culture and arts of the two countries. This was the catalyst for a successful book series on the subject called "Egyptian Yoga". Since 1999 he has researched Ancient Egyptian musical theory and created a series of musical compositions which explore this unique area of music from ancient Africa and its connection to world music.

The Limits of Faith
TABLE OF CONTENTS

PREFACE	5
THE HENOTHEISM PERIOD, THE COUNTER-REVERSION ERA, THE ASSURANCE AGE AND THE FORMATION OF WESTERN RELIGION	7
HOW THE RELIGIOUS FAR RIGHT BECAME SO EXTREME AND WHAT IS ITS POLITICAL AGENDA?	26
A Brief History of the Origins of Israel as a Jewish State	26
PASSOVER AND THE DANGER OF RELIGIOUS HEGEMONY AND RELIGIOUS ABSENTMINDEDNESS	45
PASSOVER-PART 2	56
CHRISTIAN COLLEGES AND UNIVERSITIES	68
PROSPECTS FOR THE FUTURE: RELIGION POLITICS, AND ECONOMICS IN THE 21ST CENTURY	71
The Religious Crisis	71
THE WESTERN WAY OF SEEKING FOR MEANING	83
SEEDS OF CONFLICT EMBEDDED IN THE HOLY SCRIPTURES	86
RECONCILIATION AND PEACE THROUGH RELIGIOUS REFORMS AND THE COMPLETE PRACTICE OF RELIGION	94
Arab and Muslim Conquest of Egypt and the Schism between Judaism and Christianity and Between Judaism, Christianity and Islam	98
IS REASON BORN OUT OF FAITH OR DOES FAITH COME OUT OF REASON?	103
I OR THOU?	106
THE SEARCH FOR REALITY	109
THE MEANING OF EVANESCENCE FAITH IN TECHNOLOGY AND "DOES SCIENCE ONLY IMPROVE?"	122
SCIENCE, FAITH OR THE TRANSCENDENTAL? THE DEBATE OVER CREATIONISM OR EVOLUTION AND OTHER RELATED ISSUES.	129
THE THEORY OF EVOLUTION, THE CONFLICT WITH HISTORICAL RELIGION AND A CORRECT PATH TO KNOWING	151
Q & A	157
NOTES	161
INDEX	164

The Limits of Faith

PREFACE

Faith *n.* <u>*Christianity.*</u> The theological virtue defined as secure belief in God and a trusting acceptance of God's will.

n 1: a strong belief in a supernatural power or powers that control human destiny; "he lost his faith but not his morality" [syn: religion, religious belief]
  - <u>Source:</u> *The American Heritage® Dictionary of the English Language, Fourth Edition*

Faith is in general the <u>persuasion of the mind that a certain statement is true</u> (Phil. 1:27; 2 Thess. 2:13). <u>Its primary idea is trust.</u> A thing is true, and therefore worthy of trust. It admits of many degrees up to full assurance of faith, in accordance with the evidence on which it rests. <u>Faith is the result of teaching</u> (Rom. 10:14-17). <u>Knowledge is an essential element in all faith,</u> and is sometimes spoken of as an equivalent to faith (John 10:38; 1 John 2:3).

-Source: *Easton's 1897 Bible Dictionary*

Is faith belief in something without proof? And if so is there never to be any proof or discovery? If so what is the need of intellect? If faith is trust in something that is real is that reality historical, literal or metaphorical or philosophical? If knowledge is an essential element in faith why should there by so much emphasis on believing and not on understanding in the modern practice of religion?

This volume is a compilation of essays related to the nature of religious faith in the context of its inception in human history as well as its meaning for religious practice and relations between religions in modern times. Faith has come to be regarded as a virtuous goal in life. However, many people have asked how can it be that an endeavor that is supposed to be dedicated to spiritual upliftment has led to more conflict in human history than any other social factor?

Faith-based religion has emerged in modern times as a powerful and dynamic form of social process that affects every human being as well as life in general, the animals, plants and the earth's elements. It relates to the survival of cultures as well as the survival of life itself. Thus it is important to understand what faith is and how it operates in the mind and the process that has ensued to form the world we see today.

Therefore, this volume is dedicated to the exploration of history, politics, theology and philosophy in order to comprehend and effectively realize the effects of faith and discover the means to purify faith so as to direct ourselves towards harmony, peace and prosperity for all humanity.

I have written many books on religious philosophy. This book is special in that it investigates this form of religious practice (faith-based) in one small but comprehensive volume. It also contains extensive questions and answers about this issue of faith-based religious practice. Questions have a special way of eliciting wisdom that does not come in ordinary lectures or writings. Therefore, the extensive Q & A sections of this volume should be a help to promote understanding of this difficult and often conflict producing aspect of religious practice in the modern world.

The Limits of Faith

The Henotheism Period, The Counter-Reversion Era, the Assurance Age and the Formation of Western Religion

Henotheism Period

During the sixth century B.C.E. there was a special age in human history, which some authors have termed "Axial age" due to its role in history that may be likened to an axis upon which many events turned. However, that period may be better described as a religious *"Counter-Reversion Era."* The name Counter-Reversion Era was chosen because it describes a time when the religious philosophy of the past [time before that era] was in decline due to the emergence of barbarism and certain religious movements emerged to counter that decline and revert back to the original *perennial philosophy*[1] of religion. During that time, there were several wars of conquest in which several nations in the Middle East developed into conquering forces. Some examples include the Persians and the Assyrians. That period marked a time when the power of Ancient Egypt, which had previously controlled the land areas from present day Sudan to India at one time in the past, reached its lowest state. Ancient Egypt was under constant siege during that period. However, Egypt did not experience a religious *Counter-Reversion Era*. The Ancient Egyptian religion was a purveyor of the perennial philosophy, the religious tradition of henotheism and panentheism that continued to be practiced openly until the 5th century A.C.E. [1,000 years later] when the Roman Orthodox Christians closed the last Egyptian temples by force.[2] Ancient Egypt had been the beacon of learning and science as well as spiritual wisdom. This is why the ancient pre-Judaic, pre-Christian and pre-Islamic religions had many areas of compatibility with Ancient Egyptian religion and some even included Ancient Egyptian gods and goddesses in their pantheon of divinities. The time prior to the *Counter-*

Reversion Era was marked by the practice of henotheism {In philosophy and religion, is a term coined by Max Müller, which means devotion to a single God while accepting the existence of other Gods.} and in a more developed format, pantheism {a doctrine identifying the Deity with the universe and its phenomena; belief in and worship of all gods and goddesses as manifestations of the one Supreme Being} and panentheism {the Creator is creation and transcends creation}.

The Counter-Reversion Era

The *Counter-Reversion Era* covers a period circa the 6th century B.C.E. The philosophies that emerged at that time, such as Pythagoreanism, Buddhism, Jainism, Taoism, and Confucianism had common aspects that hearkened back to and admonished the need to return to a philosophy of mystical spirituality, community service and ethics, such as was taught by the Ancient Egyptians for several thousands of years. Those philosophies, except in Greece, developed in a personalized form, with a personal leader in the form of a realized and or ascended master at its center, as opposed to the priestly format of Ancient Egypt. Ancient Egyptian religion was originally personality based [Ex. God Ra, God Osiris (Asar) or Goddess Isis (Aset)]; however, those personalities did not interfere with the capacity for the practitioners to attain high religious development since the systems introduced by those personalities were based on mystical philosophy with henotheistic components. Therefore, even though the religions that came in during the *Counter-Reversion Era* had specific founding teachers [personalities upon which the religions were based: *Pythagoras, Buddha, Mahavira, Lao-Tzu, Confucius*], their philosophies pointed to mysticism and the perennial philosophy that had existed before and led people to turn away from violence and towards cooperative peaceful coexistence and a personal quest for enlightenment by discovering the nature of self which transcends the phenomenal and which is essentially a part of the immortal, transcendental Divine, concepts that predated the inception of the new religions and philosophies.

Judaism was practiced in ancient times to the extent that the Torah [the main original Jewish religious texts] is believed by scholars to have been read publicly since the time of Ezra (c. 450 B.C.E. –after the *Counter-Reversion Era*).[3] However, at that time, Judaism did not have the Rabbinical Jewish principles of absolute monotheism as we may understand its practice today which rejects all gods and recognizes only one. At this time, Judaism accepted the henotheistic concept, which means devotion to a single god while accepting the existence of other gods. However, after the Babylonian conquest of Jerusalem, the Jews (people of Judah, part of the land ruled by the kings Saul, David, Solomon and their descendants)[4] scattered to Egypt and to Babylonia. The Egyptian Jews continued to practice the earlier form of Judaism but the Babylonian Jews started to innovate the philosophical tenets of Judaism as a reaction to the debacle caused by the Babylonian destruction of Jerusalem and the Jewish Temple in 586 B.C.E.[5] It is possible that the Babylonian Jews could have come into contact with practitioners of the Zoroastrian tradition at this time. The Babylonian exile period began to set in motion changes in Jewish religion that came to fruition in the next pivotal period of religion in the Middle East that was to have far-reaching effects on Christianity and the rest of Western culture in the 1st and 2nd millenniums A.C.E.

The Coming of the Assurance Age

> "What is now called the Christian religion has existed among the Ancients and was not absent from the beginning of the human race until Christ came in the flesh from which time the true religion which was already in existence began to be called Christian."
>
> St. Augustine (354-430 A.C.E.)

The statement by St. Augustine reveals the admission by early Christian officials that Christianity was nothing new in the sense of its original tenets. This demonstrates the tactic of cooptation through which the Christian officials worked actively to stop the practice of other religions by adopting their traditions and rituals while renaming them as Christian, a process known as co-optation. What did change was the move in Judaism and Christianity towards orthodoxy and faith-based religious practice, supported by literalism, historicity and militarism. Teachings such as the Satan and the apocalyptic notions seem to have come from Zoroastrian influences, but the concepts of the resurrection, the Eucharist, the cross symbol, the 14 Stations of the Cross, the concept of the good shepherd, and many others, came directly from Ancient Egyptian religion.

During the early part of the 1st millennium A.C.E., 500 to 700 years after the Counter-Reversion Era, during the period of 70 A.C.E. to 300 A.C.E., a new age emerged that was characterized by the need for certainty or assurance in spiritual practice. This period was marked by wars, national violence and tyranny imposed by the Romans on most other groups at the time, thus forcing upon them harsh conditions and fomenting the creation of religious zealots.[6] The Jewish people lived in Egypt and Palestine and were all under the domination of the Roman Empire, especially after the destruction of the Jewish Temple in c. 70 A.C.E. At that time, there were four main sects of Judaism. These comprised what is referred to as the "Jewish People" or followers of the Jewish religion who were, culturally and ethnically speaking, Hebrews. The sects were: *Pharisees, Sadducees, Essenes* and the *Zealots,* and they were known to have individuals who claimed to be Messiahs, who were fighters and preachers that led revolts against the Romans and were revered as liberators —many years before Jesus of the Christian religion was supposed to have existed. Each of these groups affected the development of the Jewish scriptures until the time when the Canonization of the Hebrew Bible was essentially complete in c. 90-150 A.C.E.[7]

In this period, the search for certainty meant a move away from the apparent uncertainty of mysticism and mystical philosophy to the simplicity and apparent certainty of faith and belief systems. Religion changed from a discipline dedicated to promoting experience of the Divine to a dogmatic system of believing in or having faith in a particular form of Divine. In essence, the religious practice became synonymous with faith in belief itself. This was the beginning of the *Assurance Age* which still continues in those parts of the world affected by the religions that developed in the Middle East that are today known as Zoroastrianism, Judaism, Christianity and Islam.

Zoroastrianism also developed during the same *Counter-Reversion Era* period (6th century B.C.E.), but its tenets were somewhat different than the other religions of the *Counter-Reversion Era* previously mentioned. Zoroastrianism was a departure from henotheism and is often touted as the first monotheistic religion, though it contained within it a dualistic format with divinities of good and evil and the expectation of a great final battle at the end of time, which is a henotheistic format. The concept of the dual opposing forces can be found, for example, in the Heru (Horus)-Set concept of Ancient Egypt and the Yin-Yang of Chinese Taoism. Yet, the preeminence of the Supreme Being, situated as an exclusive and special divinity in Zoroastrianism was a departure from the pantheistic model that would see the Zoroastrian Supreme Being as a manifestation with equal value as the Supreme Being in say, Judaism.

The history of religions and cultures besides Ancient Egypt in the period prior to the 6th century B.C.E. is recognized generally by historians as uncertain, though it is known that previously mentioned religions [Judaism, Christianity] had no notions of divinities of evil such that could be equated with or regarded as a "devil." However, religious scholarship has demonstrated that Judaism was not orthodox in the sense of following the particular dogma of monotheism as we know it today. At its inception and up to the rabbinic period, Judaism practiced henotheism. When the earlier Jewish conceptions are examined more closely, they reveal a closer affinity to the Ancient Egyptian model that follows the traditional African model of a Supreme Being that is transcendental, with lesser beings that operate effectively in Creation [henotheism]. In fact, the Jews that moved back to Egypt believed their main god, Jehova [Hebrew: *YHWH*], to be *"Yahou who is in Elephantine"*[8] Elephantine is the city in Upper (southern) Egypt today known as "Aswan." This ancient city was the residence of the Ancient Egyptian god Khnum, the Creator.

The early Jewish [non-rabbinic] concept describes the Creation in terms of an act of sexual union. *Elohim* (Ancient Hebrew for gods/goddesses) impregnates the primeval waters with *ruach,* a Hebrew word which means *spirit*, *wind* or the verb *to hover*. The same word means *to brood* in Syriac. Elohim, also called El, was a name used for God in some Hebrew scriptures.[9] Therefore, the original Jewish concept incorporates gods and goddesses within the understanding of a central source divinity in accordance with the previous models of religion and their form of the "theological religious framework" or "God Framework" that was used to determine the religious dogma and relationship between God or Spirit and Human beings.

When the Jewish Temple was destroyed in 70 A.C.E. by the Romans, the Jews were scattered and apparently had contact with practitioners of Zoroastrianism and there ensued a new movement in Jewish religion called "Rabbinic Judaism." This period also marked the first Christian writings [Gospels and Letters of Paul 70 A.C.E.-100 A.C.E.] as Christianity developed into a sect of Judaism. Both Judaism and

The Limits of Faith

Christianity followed the teachings contained in the Jewish Torah. The term Torah, means "to teach" in Hebrew, and is strictly the first five books of the Old Testament, which are *Genesis, Exodus, Leviticus, Numbers*, and *Deuteronomy* containing laws and customs of Judaism. They are sometimes referred to as the Jewish Bible or the Pentateuch. Moses is generally claimed as the author, having received inspiration from God on Mt Sinai.[10] There were different sects of Christianity, including the Gnostics and the Orthodox.

During the period of Rabbinic Judaism, the rabbis were seeking to reinterpret Jewish practices and concepts as the people were in exile, and at a time when the Temple was not in existence (destroyed) and there was no anchor for Jewish practice.[11] Prior to the development of the Rabbinic Judaism form of Judaism, Jewish practice included a henotheistic view of Divinity as discussed above. The same was true in Gnostic Christianity. However, with the development of Rabbinic Judaism, there developed the concept of exclusive monotheism that was different from the henotheistic form of monotheism. The Rabbinical movement held that there is only one main god as opposed to the previous view that there was one main god among other lesser gods, which was included in the Ancient Egyptian religions, African religions, Greek religions and Indian religions. Besides the Jewish Torah text, the Talmud was developed. The Talmud is a collection of rabbinical writings that were interpretations of the Torah to explain the Torah scriptures and how to apply the Torah teachings. Scholars assign the date of creation and writing of the Talmud as being between the years of the second and fifth centuries A.C.E. However, Orthodox Jews assign it to an earlier date through oral tradition and thus believe it was revealed to Moses at the same time as the Torah, but was preserved orally until the time it was codified by being written down. So the Talmud is regarded as an "Oral Torah," and the Torah or Tanakh is referred to as the "Written Torah."[12]

When Christianity separated from Judaism, now believing in the Old Testament {Jewish Torah} and also the Christian writings that were later compiled into a "New Testament," and when orthodox Christianity was adopted by the Roman emperors, a form of Christianity that tended towards the universal law or application [catholic] and strict monotheism, as well as male superiority, came into power. Thus, Rabbinic Judaism and Roman Catholic Christianity developed their philosophy by adopting certain Zoroastrian principles that they did not have previously. Rabbinic Judaism also developed a universalistic perspective (that the Torah contained universal truths). Here universalism comes to signify that these truths are universal in the sense that they are real and correct and applicable to all, while other teachings may be speculations, but are certainly less than universal and therefore limited and thus not correct. Rabbinic Judaism came into existence after the destruction of the second Jewish Temple in Jerusalem in 70 A.C.E., but had its main development period from the second to sixth centuries A.C.E. By the time of the sixth century, Rabbinic Judaism had become established as the normative [dominant- standard] form of Judaism.

Some examples of tenets adopted by Judaism from Zoroastrianism include:

> ➢ A tangible, active force for evil (Angra Mainyu, whose attributes were assumed by the later Jewish Satan).
> ➢ Concept of a final judgment of souls after death.
> ➢ Concept of the afterlives in heaven or hell.

Scholars believe that it was possible that the Jews heard those teachings during the period at the end of the Babylonian Exile, under the Persian emperor Cyrus.[13] Prior to the period referred to as the Babylonian captivity (586-538 B.C.E.), Jewish philosophy held that Satan was an agent of God and that he tested man's loyalty to God. Sometime after *Cyrus the Great* permitted the Jews to return to Jerusalem, Satan became the personification of evil, a personality wherein evil originated. Therefore, in this new view, evil was not in human beings, but outside of them. It was not inherent or potential, say due to ignorance, error or volition, but it was an effect of association with Satan and therefore, anything Satanic must be evil and avoided, if not destroyed. Thus, anything in contradiction to the teaching is Satanic and therefore, to be repudiated, and if possible, eradicated. The danger of this kind of philosophy should be noted. Anything that the leaders did not like or that contradicted them could be deemed satanic and therefore evil. Consider the examples of the Spanish inquisition and the Salem Witch trials. This kind of philosophy facilitates closed mindedness and fundamentalist repudiation of anything new or different. Thus, Satan became lord of evil and God's rival.

The Limits of Faith

According to Nesta Ramazani, "Islamic institutions such as *waqf* (religious endowments) and *madreseh* (a theological school attached to a mosque) have their roots in Zoroastrian traditions".[14] However, the concept of Angra Mainyu of Zoroastrianism is not exactly the same as Satan because Angra Mainyu {evil} with Spenta Mainyu {good} were two aspects that came together to complement each other into a whole within Ahura Mazda, the Supreme Being. In Christianity, Satan is a lesser being, but may be seen as complementary to Jesus in the philosophical understanding as complementary opposites. However, present Jewish and Christian practice would see Satan as an abomination and completely separate from God and not as an agent of God, even though he served a purpose in tempting Jesus [in the Christian gospel accounts] and thus testing his resolve. So, attributes from Zoroastrianism were adopted for the Satan character. The dualistic battle of good versus evil in the New Testament was adopted from Zoroastrianism and figures prominently in the Book of Revelation and in Apocalyptic literature.

The henotheistic religions of the pre-Assurance Age were associated with mysticism, pantheism and panentheism. A mystical religion does not require belief in a dogma above practices that promote virtue. Rather, an experience-based religion [mysteries, pantheistic, panentheistic] initially requires faith in the practice of the disciplines that promote purity of body and virtue [purity of heart]. The mystical practitioner should believe in the philosophy of the spiritual practice and develop an understanding of the nature of the Divine and when the actual experience of communion and unity with the divine occurs, the belief turns into experience and the faith is fulfilled. Thus, the faith is not perpetual or an end in itself in the mystical religion; it has a purpose that is to be achieved while alive and not just after death. Having experienced the Divine, there is no need for faith since the practitioner can rely on memory and experience. The mystical practitioner can believe in himself or herself as the source of Divinity, and can also recognize that same Divinity in nature and transcending Creation, but in mysticism practice, the practitioner learns to transcend the idea of self as ego, to expand beyond the limited concept of self as a finite personality. The mystic would learn that he/she is part of the vast and unfathomable essence of the universe which is *unnamable and un-definable and un-circumscribable*. The mystic learns that gods and goddesses are metaphors to explain the nature of Divinity, so male and female divinities express the duality of existence that is resolved in the unity of human and Divine: the individual soul and universal Spirit. In mysticism, God can be approached as a personality, but is not a considered as a particular personality or as confined to a particular form, but rather, as the very essence of all that is perceived and that which transcends what is perceived. In mystical religion, God is understood as the essence of all, including the human soul. Therefore, every soul is one with God essentially. Humans have forgotten that essential nature. The discipline of mysticism is to rediscover that essential nature. Therefore, even the notion of a Supreme Being and lesser gods and goddesses is to be transcended in the mystical practice. This concept within the Ancient Egyptian Mysteries {*Shetaut Neter*} was called *Sema* in Ancient Egypt, and *Yoga* in post Aryan India. The advanced mystic learns that he/she is not limited except through ignorance of their true nature. In fact, they discover that they are one with the universe and with the Transcendental Self (God, Divinity) and transcending even the concept of God.

So due to all those intricate and multifaceted mystical concepts *Transcendental Divinity, being one with God, indefinable, inexact, etc.,* mystical religion would be perceived by the dogmatic, faith-based-assurance seeking religions of the first and second centuries A.C.E. [Judaism and Christianity], as difficult, indeterminate, or ambiguous, and therefore inexact and incorrect, and thus wrong.

Mystical philosophy requires some degree of reflective intellectual capacity. The strife of that period left less time for philosophizing about the nature of self and the universe. Therefore, a more simplified format of religion was desired. Such a religion would be more easily adopted by the masses and would offer more of a feeling of certainty or assurance to its believers to meet their more immediate needs, like salvation from the Romans. For example, the Gnostic (mystical Christianity) concept of Christ Consciousness as found in the Gnostic Gospel of Thomas [not included in the canonical Christian bible] is that any individual can attain that state of spiritual elevation. This would also mean that all are potentially daughters and sons of God, and not just Jesus. Furthermore, all can be one with God. But that attainment requires philosophical inquiry into the nature of self. In the faith-based religion, there is no admittance of a human being to a beatific state of consciousness; that idea would be seen as blasphemy. In the dogmatic Christian religion, there is only one Christ

The Limits of Faith

and only he has Christ Consciousness, and salvation after death comes from believing in him. The best that a believer can hope for is being resurrected to live with God in heaven. So, in the mysticism-based religious practice, there is need for ethical purity as well as philosophy and spiritual research to discover the mysteries of life for oneself; all of that requires time and self-effort spent in working on oneself to transform oneself. In the faith-based religion, there is no need for research since all answers are known and recorded in "the book" [bible] and all that is necessary is to believe in the book. Here there is no time needed beyond attendance at regular worship meetings to reaffirm the faith basis of the religion. That attendance in itself is evidence of keeping faith, and therefore the goal of the religion is achieved.

In a religion based on faith, that faith requires and demands belief first and foremost. It cannot tolerate disbelief, because without belief there is no religion being practiced. The required belief is conviction in the dogma of the existence of a concrete Creator God who created physical human beings, a concrete universe and who exists as a separate entity somewhere in the universe and is watching constantly the individual human beings who have limited personalities and have no direct connection to God or to nature, but who will be taken physically to heaven to exist with God for eternity if they follow his laws and have faith in him.

Since the culture that it emerged from was caught in a struggle for survival, in fear of being put to death, and finding itself readying itself often for war and zealous confrontation against the powers that were in existence at the time, threatening it, the people and the faith-based religion became closely associated with fear and survival issues, and therefore, that fear transferred to fear of God. This means that the faith itself was under constant challenge. The Christian response to the Romans or to disbelievers was not through philosophy, but through simple dogmas about the faith. The simplest and most important dogma is the dogma of having faith in God or Jesus, so as to be resurrected when Jesus comes back. Therefore, the faith was the focus of interest, not the substance of the faith in and of itself.

This kind of religious practice is closely focused on the personality of God and not the essential nature and commonality of the human essence with God's essence. Therefore, the faith-based practice is heavily focused on

The Limits of Faith

the actions of God in terms of human understanding of human activities. Thus, just as humans can seek revenge or retribution on other people or punish their children, so too God is seen as ready to punish people if they deviate from a prescribed path that God has supposedly laid out.

How could the Jewish path be the correct path to salvation if there are other religions with different paths and those people are also seeking salvation? The answer would be that the Jewish path must be the only path and all others are false paths. Practitioners of the faith-based religion are concerned more with God's power and capacity for retribution instead of his power for compassion and love. These forms of religion, having adopted the idea of universalism [teaching applies to all] developed the tradition, especially in Christianity, of requiring the conversion of those who are unbelievers in order to sure up the faith [make certain], that is, make the religion universal and therefore absolute.

Since there can be only one absolute, that necessarily means that all other religions are false because unlike the faith-based religion which is supposedly historical and literal, the other religions are mythic, and therefore metaphorical, and not literal or historical, which renders them untrue in a phenomenal sense. So the ideal in a faith-based religion is faith in an historical certainty since reality and history must coexist. Therefore, the religion of certainty must also be historical as well as literal, because the writings cannot be historical and accurate without being literally true. Conversely, they cannot be literally true without also being historical true. Thus, all histories that contradict that literal and historical view of religion are false or heretical.

Since in dogmatic faith-based Judaism and Christianity, those who believe in heresies or who do not come to the "true religion" are going to hell, they may be considered as less than human. This means also that faith or belief without application can be accepted as religious practice. In other words, one can say one believes in the Christian faith and be considered "Christian," but that does not require one to act in accordance with any ethical or moral regulation since faith in itself is the religion. This feature of dogmatic [doctrinaire, authoritarian, rigid] religions is evinced in the Christian Church emphasis on expressions of faith, but not of virtue, and the Jewish Temple's emphasis on ritual and tradition as opposed to virtue. This would mean that even if a person were to act like Jesus or in a

The Limits of Faith

manner that is prescribed by the Old Testament, but the person is not a believer in Judaism or Christianity that person would be considered as a non-believer by the Jews and Christians. For example, Mahatma Gandhi, a follower of Hinduism and a person who upheld the same ethical principles as Jesus would not be considered a Christian, and therefore would be going to hell because "he did not believe." The same can be said for the other major faith-based religion of our time Islam, which also expresses that its God (Allah) is the only God, and thus the only true God, its religion is the only true religion, the Koran is the only true scripture, and those who do not follow Islam (unbelievers) will go to hell for all eternity; Islam has its roots Judaism and Christianity.

The emphasis of the faith-based religion on faith as a criterion for determining who is a follower of the religion is evinced in the manner in which "sinners" are treated by the religion. A person who claims to be a believer who has attempted and failed in upholding the regulations of the religion is still accepted as a member of the religion. For example, a person who commits adultery has failed in upholding the commandment against adultery, but is not thrown out of the church. Thus, there is a clear implication that faith is more important than virtue. The contradiction in this arises in the case of homosexuality; there are many religious right wing Christian groups that would expel homosexuals, instead of forgive {if it is a sin} and accept them, which is a form of duplicitous treatment, since the adulterer would be accepted and forgiven even though adultery is more prominently mentioned in the bible and should therefore be considered as a greater sin {if it is a sin}. There are many mainstream Christians who may say that they do not support that hard-line on sinners such as homosexuals or adulterers, but support by mainstream Christians of Christianity in general also supports the right wing Christians, and because they have more political power, the mainstream Christians are supporting their political agenda.

This concept, of emphasis on faith instead of virtue is perhaps epitomized in the Christian notion of confession wherein a person can be absolved of sins by merely telling a priest about them or by "sincerely" repenting just before death. This concept is rejected in the non-faith-based religions since there is recognition that a person's character is composed of longstanding egoistic desires that must be purified through virtuous deeds over time. Those who treat religion in the way of having faith but also committing unethical acts such as stealing [from mugging to white collar crime], graft, assassination, war, subjugation of other peoples through imperialist tactics, lynching, rape, child molestation, adultery, etc., are often accused of practicing religion in name only, yet that is the logical extension of the faith-based religious philosophical idea, to just believe.

Fundamentalists might say that the instructions of the Bible must be practiced literally. Yet, how would *an eye for an eye* {Old Testament} be reconciled with *turn the other cheek* {New Testament}? The contradictions of such concepts coupled with the dogmatic demand to blind faith often has lead to imperfection of practice as evinced in the downfall of Catholic priests who have been convicted of child molestation or other crimes, or of such prominent evangelical preachers as Jimmy Swaggart and Jim Baker whose ministries collapsed due to egregious sins as defined by their religions. Yet those individuals were forgiven and accepted as Christians. Some have manifested patently un-Christian behavior such as the viciousness of promoting the assassination of foreign leaders or praying for the death of Supreme Court Justices who may not support the right wing religious right political agenda, as Pat Robertson did. This reflects the extreme application of exclusivist and universalistic notions that permeate the faith-based religion that in effect cancels out or invalidates virtue or ethics in the pursuit of what is considered by the religion as greater, i.e. faith. Therefore, sinful behavior can be excused by the religion if the person claims to be Christian; also, crime and unethical behavior can be excused by the religion if the person claims to be Christian and the acts are portrayed as upholding the faith. So killing, making war or crimes in the name of upholding the religion are acceptable; the example of that concept is evinced in the decrees of the Pope advocating the Crusades, in today's Christians making war on other nations, and in the corporations of Christians, Jews and Muslims exploiting other peoples around the world. Consequently, if it is acceptable to commit crimes in the support of faith, why not commit crimes in support of king or country or family? Is it not necessary to support the family so it can support the church or temple? This line of logic has been presented to demonstrate the subconscious or unconscious or even conscious mental operations that can form the basis for the amorality and cruelty that can manifest from practitioners of faith-based religions, and have led to wars as well as oppression on "nonbeliever" groups, i.e., persons who do not follow that particular religion.

The Limits of Faith

That confusion in traditional Christianity opens the door for uncertainty, so criticisms are often answered either by calls to believe faithfully and not question the "word of God" because there must be some higher wisdom in those scriptures, or the critic may be attacked as an unbeliever or a hell-bound devil worshipper, who was sent to test the faithful believers, or who should be excommunicated and ignored or discredited for being a follower of rationality instead of faith.

That inability or unwillingness to face criticism or apply critical thinking to the scriptural tenets maintains the religion as a faith-based rather than rational practice. Devoid of rationality, the faith-based religion must eventually resort to violent repudiation of that which is or which it believes is criticizing the faith-based dogma as evil and attempting to lure the faithful to ruin. Therefore, the faith-based religion must always be alert to reject criticism as well as contradictory ideas. The challenging ideas are not responded to with rational counterarguments by the faith-based religious practitioners; they are answered with exhortations to have faith. That form of answer closes off debate and negates the need or even discourages critical thinking and spiritual inquiry. When religious zealots or demagogues are able to control the masses of fanatical faith-based religious followers, the consequences can be calamitous because the leader can claim to be divinely inspired, and since no proof is required beyond the appearance of being touched by the spirit, which can be faked by any skilled con artist, the followers can be manipulated into accepting or partaking in heinous crimes against humanity.

In mystical practice, the practitioner is not forced to have faith in a teaching or a teacher or to convert others. All come to that in the fullness of their spiritual development. In experience-based (mystical) religions, the followers are not forced to believe in certain personalities as means to achieve their salvation through those personalities. In mystical religion, the spiritual seeker is admonished to trust in the teaching and the teacher until they are able to experience the truth of the teaching for themselves. In mystical religion, the spiritual seeker is not pushed to convert others or condemn others who do not follow the same tradition; all follow the paths they are suited to due to their previous desires, feelings and ethical character. A true teacher of mysticism, a Sage or enlightened being, is recognized by mystics as they cleanse their personalities from un-virtuous aspects of character. They essentially discover who is an authentic philosopher by becoming philosophers themselves, by questioning and then practicing the disciplines of the mystical teachings.

Conclusion

What caused the two main religions [Judaism and Christianity] to turn from henotheism to faith-based religion which concentrates on assurance, certainty, historicity and literalism? These developments [move towards zealotry and dogmatism as well as faith-basis instead of experience-basis in religious practice] may be seen as a reaction to extreme violence and holocaust type experiences at the hands of the Babylonians or Romans. So this means that the extreme violence of the Romans drew a reaction in the form of extreme dogmatism from the Christians. Those religious practitioners were in search of concrete answers to their miseries and immediate salvation from their suffering. So in order to confront the juggernaut of the Roman Empire, the counterbalance was the creation of a concretized religious philosophy founded upon the idea of a physical liberator and a physical and final end to the great misery that was being suffered. The apocalyptic vision of Zoroastrianism, which was not originally part of the Judeo-Christian tradition as such, fit into that need.

Additionally, the reliance on historicity and literalism could have the effect of impressing potential followers and luring them away from other religions that were not historically based, and therefore more easily relegated to not being true. In a sense, orthodox religion may be seen as a spiritual representation of imperial culture since it, like the political empire, seeks to control and dictate to all the peoples within its domain, what they are to think and believe and do, and just as the empire will relate peacefully to its people as long as the people do what they are told, so too the faith-based religions are peaceful towards those followers who believe, but hostile to those people who do not. Just as the empire seeks to expand and conquer all, the faith-based orthodox religion must convert all. In another sense the faith-based religions are reactions to the barbarism of their times. Just as the Roman Empire treated them with extreme violence, the faith-based religion must practice religion with an equal measure of zealotry that can leave no unbelievers in peace.

The Limits of Faith

The barbarism of the Romans was matched by the zeal of the zealots who adopted a diametrically opposed ideology in religious terms to the position of the Roman polytheism. Another factor polarizing religion was the competition between polytheism, as it was understood by the orthodox Christians, and their own conception of absolute monotheism. The orthodox Christians regarded the henotheistic religions of their time [Ancient Egyptian, Indian, Greek, etc.] as polytheism. In fact, henotheism is not the same as polytheism, and philosophically speaking, is therefore not a diametrically opposed concept to monotheism, because in a way henotheism accommodated the monotheistic concept in the framework of a central figure around which peripheral entities are found. It is not unlike the metaphor of the sun and the planets, but it is actually even closer to the Christian concept of God and the angels and saints, because the concept of angels and saints developed out of the earlier pre-Judeo-Christian traditions. Yet, the dogmatic faith-based followers can accept nothing that is not what they perceive as exactly the same as their concept. That struggle fomented the polarization of that sect of Jews [Christians] that moved them away from their own traditional henotheistic beliefs. This development had a strong effect on the entirety of Jewish religious philosophy and practice.

The intense misery of life can operate to prevent intellectual and mystically oriented thought processes; it creates insensitivity to the subtleties of human experience and promotes hardheartedness and the ideal of concrete [faith] instead of abstract [philosophical] thinking. The predilection towards faith alone as the basis of religious practice discourages deeper religious experiences, and hence people come to believe they have the religious experience through expressions of faith instead of expressions of inner spiritual discovery beyond the concrete personality. This same principle applies to the predilection in Western countries towards a mechanistic and scientific way of thinking about human development as epitomized in the Cartesian concept of a mechanistic universe [Descartes' reductionistic view was that everything can be dismantled and studied in parts (like a machine) in order to understand the whole] or the mechanistic view of the human body in medical science that persists to this day through allopathic medical practice which repudiates alternative or traditional medical practices that may be just as or more effective. This tendency is also evident in the ideal

The Limits of Faith

of Western art that revered "realism" instead of the abstract or folkloric forms of art.

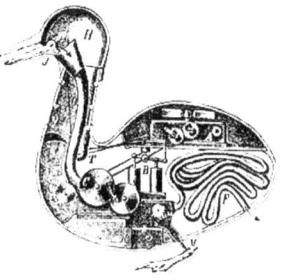

Descartes held that - contrary to humans - animals could be reductively explained as automata - *De homines 1622)*

Certainly not all followers of faith-based religions are insensitive and unvirtuous, or uninterested in virtue or a more ecumenical or all-inclusive practice of religion. However, the framework of those religions is designed to promote that form of religious practice that is narrow-minded, fanatical, blind, fearful and intolerant. Therefore, the most fanatical elements of that form of religion actually do reflect the highest perspective enjoined by the traditional form of practice that the religion has developed based on its original tenets. Under those conditions, those who may consider themselves as moderates or marginal believers could be shamed [coerced] into supporting the more zealous proponents, and thereby the zealots would have power to control the actions of the majority.

On May 2, 2006 Madeline Albright made some critical comments about President George W. Bush on *"The Daily Show with John Stewart."* She noted that at a recent meeting between former Secretaries of State and Defense that President George Bush was not seeking advice, but instead issued policy statements. She added, [Highlighted text by Ashby]

> I went back and looked at a lot of America's history and most of our presidents have invoked God in some form or another, what is different about president Bush is that <u>he is so certain about his religion</u>, none of the doubts that president Lincoln raised and I think then what happens is it makes people wonder whose on the other side and anybody who picks a fight with us is picking a fight with God, which is why he has made this so difficult and complicated.

The Limits of Faith

President George W. Bush has made statements about how he prays and is guided by God. In reply to Albright's statement, John Stewart said that he thought *"that God would be doing a better job in Iraq,"* referring to the deteriorating war that the president chose to start. In reference to the faled policy related to the war in Iraq, Albright added,

> ...there was no planning for the next part [the occupation of Iraq] and you had Secretary [Colin] Powel on who was explaining that and I think that is the real problem, there was an expectation there would be dancing in the streets and part of the problem about being so certain that you are getting the message is you never have a plan "B". All the Bush administration went in was plan "A", everyone would love us, and no idea about plan "B" and the looting and the fact that we would be viewed as occupyers and not as liberators.

The reaction by Madeline Albright is typical of several people who have met with the president and have indicated that he seems not to listen to advice. At the White House Correspondent's dinner of 2006, comedian Stephen Colbert noted that the president *"held on to the same opinion on Wednesday that he had on Monday no matter what happened on Tuesday."* That intractable grasp unto the political or religious dogma denotes a strongly dogmatic personality, a person who holds on to the dogma regardless of any contradictory information. The obstinate grasp on to the projected reality and the certainty of his convictions indicate, again, a personality that is inflexible and whose ideas or deeply held notions are hard to shake. Therefore, such a personality cannot learn from mistakes or improved ways of doing things, because they are new and conflict with the accepted absolute beliefs. This is why also such a personality can say one policy for the benefit of others and follow another, closer to the deeply held belief. The current U.S.A. president, George W. Bush, thus presents an extreme example of the religious dogmatic leader that can pose a significant threat to peace, as such a personality would find great difficulty in accepting any reality not in accord with its own beliefs. The assessment by Albright confirms the denied statements (see below) by George W. Bush, which confirm his mindset as a dogmatic personality, relying on religion and projecting his notion of reality, rooted in the faith-based dogma, onto the world so as to reshape it to his satisfaction, enforcing it on others, regardless of the consequences, because in his mind the alternative is worse. The following statements were reportedly said by President George W. Bush, but were later denined by the White House.

The Limits of Faith

"I'm driven with a mission from God. God would tell me, George, go and fight those terrorists in Afghanistan. And I did, and then God would tell me, George, go and end the tyranny in Iraq… And I did. And now, again, I feel God's words coming to me, go get the Palestinians their state and get the Israelis their security, and get peace in the Middle East. And by God I'm gonna do it."[15]/[16]

Some political observers and sociologists have examined the presidents actions and some have suggested that the president may not be lying from his perspective in the way that he thinks what he is saying about reality is true from the perspective of how he thinks it should be. Thus, it is indicative of a personality that looks at the world through his own prism, a deluded version of reality, based on an imaginary desired truth founded on the faith-based dogma or ideology. In any case, this vision of reality or the belief that he can reshape reality to fit his idea of reality is either shared or assisted by his advisors [recall the Ron Suskind article where he quoted one of the Bush advisors as saying: We're history's actors . . . and you, all of you, will be left to just study what we do."].[17]

The Limits of Faith

How the Religious Far Right Became so Extreme and What is its Political Agenda?

The rising fundamentalism and extremism {zealotry} of the religious right in the U.S.A. faith-based religions over the last 40 years is in part due to a fundamentalist, literal and fanatical view of the apocalyptic ideas of the Jewish-Christian bible as well as a profound fear of annihilation or being taken over by the forces of evil, the devil or Islam, etc. These pressures have fomented the emergence and expansion of extremist and irrational theological movements in the U.S.A. These movements are bound up with the creation of a Jewish state and what that supposedly means in biblical prophesies, and the desire of some to make those prophesies come true. The following comment is from Kevin Phillips, former GOP (Republican Party) Strategist.

> If you just had Jews taking up the cudgels for Israel, it wouldn't do it. What you've had from the start is that the country in Europe that was most anxious to have an Israel in the 19th century was Britain, because that's where you have – well, Disraeli was prime minister, but you had a fair Jewish community, and there was this Protestant sense of to have the biblical prophesies come true, Israel had to be restored. And in the United States, the expectations among Christian evangelicals that foreign policy should serve a biblical aspect, in other words, that this should become part of American foreign policy, it's huge…
> …What you've got is that 45% of American Christians believe in Armageddon, and the more religious ones, the fundamentalists and evangelicals more than anybody else. So, my assumption is that the Bush electorate is probably 50 to 55% people who believe in Armageddon and probably more or less the same numbers who believe that the Antichrist is already on earth.[18]

A Brief History of the Origins of Israel as a Jewish State

The Limits of Faith

Beginning with Abraham (c. 1,500 B.C.E?) and ending with the creation of a Jewish state in 1948 A.C.E., the events surrounding the land today known as Palestine and the creation of the Jewish state of Israel shows the long struggle of the Jewish people to establish a permanent country for themselves and the conflict which ensued when the Jews were successful in taking control of the land which has been considered as the Holy Land for Jews, Christians, and Muslims. The Jewish Bible relates the story of Abraham. The term Abraham, according to the Bible Book of Genesis, means in Hebrew, father of many nations or Abram (ā′ brəm) [Hebrew, exalted father]. In the Jewish Bible, he is progenitor of the Hebrews; in the Islamic Qur'an text he is recognized as ancestor of the Arabs.

> Abraham was the foremost of the Biblical patriarchs. Later in life he went by the name Abraham. There is no contemporary mention of his life, and no source earlier than Genesis mentions him, so it is difficult to know if he was a historical figure. If he was, he probably lived[19] between 2166 BC and 1991 BC.[20]

The idea of the creation of Israel, as a state, had begun in ancient times, as described in the Jewish Old Testament as God purportedly made an agreement with the Hebrews to provide them with a promised land. However, since the time when the early ancient attempts failed, it was not until recent times, the late 1800s A.C.E. that the movement took on strength due to the ability of the Jews to develop political clout and financial backing from their own sources and from the Western countries. The Zionist[21] leaders in Britain always viewed Britain as an important potential supporter in their efforts to create a Jewish state. Britain was at that time the greatest world empire and military power. Jews had been able to settle there in relative peace and security and they had been able to become part of the power elite of the country, producing such political and social leaders as Benjamin Disraeli [who actually became prime minister in 1868 and 1874] and Walter Rothschild. The Balfour Declaration of 1917, in favor of "the establishment in Palestine of a national home for the Jewish people," was crucial to the plans of the Zionist leaders. In the aftermath of World War II, when the Palestinians were weak militarily and the Western countries were stronger, Britain took control of the area. This was the opportunity that the Jewish leaders were waiting for since 1896. These factors, coupled with the Western interest in Middle Eastern oil, enabled the Jewish leaders to promote the partitioning of Palestine and obtain the permission and financing to start a settlement in Palestine. The establishment of a Jewish State was not officially part of the original settlement idea as authorized by the previous declarations of the United Nations or the British mandate. Having succeeded in settling the land, the Jews then set out to establish and expand a Jewish State by military force. [22] In order to do that, it was necessary to forcibly remove Palestinians (Arab and Muslim inhabitants). The Jews created settlements for the Palestinians, which some observers likened to Bantustans, in which the Palestinians were hemmed in and segregated from the Israeli areas and could only go there with special permits in order to work. Those actions were the first contributing factors of the current rancor between the Arabs and Jews over the Palestinian/Jewish territories. This conflict between the European Jews and others who settled the land by force and the Arab Muslims led to several wars with no resolution to the issue. Since the late 1960s, many Christian groups in the U.S.A. and Britain have supported the state of Israel, which has intensified the problem. This issue promoted anti-Western sentiment in the Islamic countries [especially in the Middle East], but became a rallying point for right wing politicians who used it as a political issue. The religious right Christian groups and AIPAC, the America Israel Public Affairs Committee, gained unprecedented lobbying power in the government that contributed to the general right wing mood of the culture of the U.S.A.[23]

Part of the religious conception of religious right Christian groups is that the Jewish state is to be supported because that is supposedly what the Bible demands, as that will help to bring about the set of events that will lead to the end times and usher in the return of Jesus and the salvation of the faithful. Therefore, that support and the coincidental agenda of the right wing conservatives, neo-conservatives and European power elites, who want to have a friendly power base in the Middle East, came together for a common goal.

The religious far right in the U.S.A. is composed of those people who believe in literal biblical or traditional fundamentalist teachings of prophecies of the Judeo-Christian Bible including the concepts of **Dominionism, Apocalypticism** and **Reconstructionism.**

The Limits of Faith

Dominionism is a term used by some social scientists and critics to describe a trend in Protestant Christian evangelicalism and fundamentalism that encourages political participation in civic society by Christians through appeals to their religious beliefs.

Politically active conservative Christians rarely use the term dominionism as a self-description; many feel it is a loaded or pejorative term. Use of the term is primarily limited to secular and leftist critics of the Christian Right. The term emerged in relation to the Christian Right in the mid-1990s, but became more widely known due in large part to the U.S. presidential election, 2004 where the media attributed Republican wins to "Evangelical" voters in "Red states" who voted for "moral values". Some poll analysts call this claim over-simplistic. It has been claimed to be a kind of Triumphalism.

Apocalypticism is a worldview based on the idea that important matters are hidden from view and they will soon be revealed in a major confrontation of earth-shaking magnitude that will change the course of history.

Apocalypticism is a frequent theme of literature, film and television. It also influences political policy through movements such as Christian Zionism, and in the dualism seen when politicians demonize and scapegoat their enemies as wholly bad, evil, or even Satanic. This process often involves conspiracism in which the apocalyptic enemy is alleged to be engaged in a conspiracy against the good or Godly people. The tendency was especially evident with the approach of the millennial year 2000, but it need not be tied to a particular calendar date.

Christian Reconstructionism is a highly controversial religious and theological movement within Protestant Christianity. Reconstructionism relates to the reconstruction of the "literal" meaning of the words of the Bible. It calls for Christians to put their faith into action in all areas of life including civil government, and envisions the private and civil enforcement of the general principles of Old Testament and New Testament moral law, including those expounded in the case laws and summarized in the Old Testament Decalogue. In Reconstructionism the idea of *godly* dominion, subject to God, is contrasted with the *autonomous* dominion of mankind in rebellion against God.[24]

Having lost the 1964 elections to the Democratic Party, the Republican Party under the direction of Paul Weirich, who was a campaign strategist, developed the idea of expanding the base of the Republican Party by targeting religious fundamentalists, Pentecostals and members of Charismatic Churches, presumably because those segments of Christianity are most closed minded because they tend to follow religion through blind faith instead of through critical thinking. In the same manner, those same sentiments could be manipulated towards blind allegiance to political leaders who seem to be upholding those fundamentalist values.

The Limits of Faith

In the 1960s, the Democratic Party sought to secularize the population and that drew a backlash from the fundamentalist religious segments of the population. The former republican strategist, Kevin Phillips explained how the religious right embraced the Republican Party, and then a strategy of using the party to acquire control of the government developed.

> Well, the rise of the religious right and the Southernization of the Republican Party has created a role of religion within the Republican Party that is unprecedented in the 20th or 21st century. And this has become a central fact, the extent to which rank-and-file Republicans have a somewhat theocratic view of what government should do and how it should ally with religion, and the extent to which the Republican Party has become the favored party of the most religious conservative segments of Protestantism, Catholicism and Judaism, where you have the Orthodox Jews in the United States turned out in such number -- and they're growing anyway, because of large families[25]

Paul Weirich coined the term Moral Majority in 1979, and that organization claimed to register nine million new voters. In the year 1981, the Council for National Policy was created to conduct secret meetings for the purpose of formulating strategies to mobilize and control the religious right politically. The council is composed of religious right leaders, gun advocates, anti-tax advocates and financers of the religious right agenda. Its first president was Tim LaHaye, the co-author of the highly successful series of books known as the "left behind series." That series of books, some of which have been made into movies, concerns a fictionalized vision, based on orthodox Christian myth and tradition, of the last days of the world in which the true believers in orthodox Christianity are taken to heaven and the other people are left behind to suffer for eternity. The following quotation reveals the views of Mr. LaHaye and the message he is putting out through the over 70 million books he has sold.

> "I myself have been a forty-five year student of the centuries-old conspiracy to use government, education, and media to destroy every vestige of Christianity within our society and establish a new world order. Having read at least fifty books on the Illuminati, I am convinced that it exists and can be blamed for many of man's inhumane actions against his fellow man during the past two hundred years." (LaHaye)[26]

It is interesting that LaHaye mentions a conspiracy to use government, education and media since that is exactly what the right wing of the Christian religion has tried to do at least since the mid 1960s. It is also interesting that he demonstrates such concerned about the Illuminati as an enemy of his group and presumably also of Christianity. The concept of denouncing an enemy, even an imaginary one, is a strategy that has been used by many groups to elicit fear in their own members so as to promote more fanaticism or zealous following. It has also been used by some groups to elicit compassion and support from others in an effort to build their ranks or for procuring donations and other considerations. Governments have used this tactic to elicit support for making war on actual or supposed enemies.

The name Illuminati was used by several groups in modern and historical times. The term Illuminati is a Latin word meaning "enlightened." The term Illuminati as it is most commonly used refers to a specific group known as the Bavarian Illuminati, which **was** a society that was founded in Germany just after 1776 A.C.E. by Adam Weishaupt, who was a professor at Ingolstadt. It was popular among the ranks of German rationalists. Rationalism [Lat.,=belonging to reason], is a philosophy, or theory which holds the concept that one can arrive at basic truth regarding the world through reason alone, without physical experience. The German Illuminati sought knowledge through disciplined thought processes of the mind. The Roman Catholic Church condemned the Illuminati and the government of Bavaria dissolved the organization in 1785 A.C.E.

In Spain and Italy in the 15th and 16th centuries A.C.E., the term *Illuminati,* or *Alumbrado,* referred to persons claiming direct communion with the Holy Spirit, asserting that outward forms of religious life are unnecessary. Their philosophy was akin to Gnosticism, the idea that one can know the Divine through mentally/spiritually experiencing oneness with the Divine. Their claims led to persecution by the Inquisition [by the church]. Other groups using the name have included the Rosicrucians, and certain followers of Jakob Boehme and Emmanuel Swedenborg.[27] So the original purpose of the Illuminati [of Spain and Italy] was to seek self-knowledge, in the tradition of the Ancient Egyptian, Indian and Greek Gnostic spiritual seekers.

It is not too difficult to understand why a Gnostic philosophy would be opposed by the church; it means bypassing interminable years worshipping in a church and paying tithes to the church without achieving higher knowledge of God versus leading life in a way that leads to independence, self-knowledge and inner experience of God without need of the church. Therefore, it is no surprise that the Illuminati in particular, and not Freemasons, would be considered as a threat, and thus be maligned.

The Freemasons did indeed achieve high positions in governments in Europe and the U.S.A. and they had a philosophy that was more compliant with Christian values, yet their "special" grouping allowed them to conspire together to affect social and economic policies through political institutions. In the present day, the Illuminati are viewed as a cabal that controls governments and economies from behind the scenes. This is of course not the same agenda as the earlier group, which followed the Gnostic path. It is well known that some of the United States' founding fathers were Freemasons, but there were unfounded suspicions of their being involved with the Illuminati because of the all-seeing pyramid in the Great Seal of the United States [see above]. That symbol was cited as an example of the Illuminati's ever-present watchful eye over Americans; however, Thomas Jefferson, on the other hand, claimed they [the Illuminati] intended to spread information and the principles of true morality. He attributed the secrecy of the Illuminati to what he called "the tyranny of a despot and priests".[28]

Thus, the Illuminati are to be considered separately from Freemasonry. The order [Freemasonry] is thought to have arisen from the English and Scottish fraternities of practicing stonemasons and cathedral builders in the early Middle Ages; traces of the society have been found as early as the 14th century. Because, however, some documents of the order trace the sciences of masonry and geometry from Egypt, Babylon, and Palestine to England and France, some historians of Masonry claim that the order has roots in antiquity.[29] While the Freemasons may claim to descend from Egypt, Babylon, and Palestine, an examination of their philosophy reveals that it does not follow precisely and faithfully the tenets of Ancient Egyptian religion, and one would not expect it to because the Christian Bible takes such a dim view of Ancient Egyptian culture,[30] and the Freemasonry's oldest extant lodge bylaws[31] cites religious toleration, loyalty to local government, and political compromise as basic to the Masonic ideal. The principles of Freemasonry supposedly enjoin liberal and democratic politics and the Masons were enjoined to believe in a Supreme Being, and to use a holy book that is appropriate to the religion of the lodge's members. Using the holy book of another religion does not follow the path of Ancient Egypt, which has its own. But the Christian church leaders would not allow any other holy book in their midst besides the Christian bible anyway. So Freemasonry was designed to be compliant to the religion of the practitioners so that they could work in other areas, while not being interfered with by the religious groups of the society. In this way it would seem that the Freemasons were the true cabal affecting the social order and that the Illuminati were used as scapegoats to deflect interest in the activities of the Freemasons. The members of the Freemason order are admonished to maintain a vow of secrecy concerning the order.

> Many of the leaders of the American Revolution, including John Hancock and Paul Revere, were members of St. Andrew's Lodge in Boston. George Washington became a Mason in 1752. At the time of the Revolution most of the American lodges broke away from their English and Scottish antecedents. Freemasonry has continued to be important in politics; 13 Presidents have been Masons, and at any given time quite a large number of the members of Congress have belonged to Masonic lodges. [32]

Thus, it is clear that from its inception the U.S.A. was founded by people who were in part followers of a secular approach to politics and economics as well as social order, even while holding a predilection for Christianity. It is those aspects of culture that upset religious fundamentalists, because without a formal theocracy it is difficult to maintain a theocratic order. In other words, the country was not founded as a theocracy even though many of its founders were avid believers in Christianity; but even though some predicted the danger of religion in politics, none would have predicted the diversity of the culture, the number of different religions that would come to the U.S.A., and the severity of the degradation of culture in relation to crime, debauchery, the scale of white collar crimes and the level of political scheming that developed since their time. Nevertheless, it would seem that a cabal of secular conservatives, the Freemasons, worked to create the social order that became the United States of America, and may even be considered as the forerunners of the present day conservatives and neo-conservatives.

Legends of other groups using the name Illuminati, whose purpose is to dominate the world, have been circulating for over a century. However, they are not a shadow conspiracy, but rather the very same persons who are trying to gain control of the world economy right now and are the ancestors of those who created slavery, flexible currency, the national banks and transnational corporations in the U.S.A. and Europe, under the guise of being religiously tolerant, loyal to government and believing in a Supreme Being. Nevertheless, today those who compose what Jeff Faux calls "The Party of Davos" [power elite-world ruling class] does not need to call itself anything because its money is the universally recognizable code that is accepted by all the power elite all over the world, regardless of language, culture, or religion and, in cases, ethnicity. Yet, some secretive organizational formats still exist, but only the power elite within those groups are part of the ruling class that controls the workings of the economy and of governments.

Many critics of the American Theocratic ideal that is espoused by right wing Christian groups that the U.S.A. was founded as a "Christian country" by Christians and so it should have Christian laws, etc., use The Treaty of Tripoli as an example of the secular political atmosphere that existed right after the creation of the United States government. The Treaty of Tripoli (also known as the Treaty of Peace and Friendship) was a treaty signed on November 4, 1796 as a peace treaty between Tripoli and the United States. The Treaty was approved by President John Adams and Secretary of State, Timothy Pickering, and ratified by the Senate of the United States on June 10, 1797. A section of the treaty is cited because it contains a statement about the religion of the United States of America in Article 11, which reads:

> "As the Government of the United States of America is not, in any sense, founded on the Christian religion; as it has in itself no character of enmity

against the laws, religion, or tranquility, of Mussulmen; and, as the said States never entered into any war, or act of hostility against any Mahometan nation, it is declared by the parties, that no pretext arising from religious opinions, shall ever produce an interruption of the harmony existing between the two countries."

This country was, at least theoretically, supposed to be a refuge for people who were being oppressed due to religious discrimination in Europe. When European settlers started emigrating to the Americas, the recent memory of religious oppression and conflict in Europe led many Europeans [ex. The Puritans[33]] to seek freedom in the Americas from the same type of religious demagoguery and intolerance as the religious right wing began to display in the late 20th and early 21st centuries in the United States. So the U.S.A. was designed to have a government that was not controlled by religious interests. Though the "founding fathers" may have envisioned religions other than the European religious sects of Christianity and Judaism in "America," they may not have envisioned the religions from other parts of the world. Nevertheless, varied members of Christian groups have tried, especially in the last 40 years, to characterize the U.S.A. as a Christian country. The tone of the country indeed became polarized; as more internal and external strife was experienced, the Christian majority turned more towards religious based ideas in relation to national politics and foreign policies.

In the year 1988, Rev. Pat Robertson[34] founded The Christian Coalition after losing his run for the presidency. The Christian Coalition of America is a U.S.A. Christian political advocacy group, which includes Christian fundamentalists, Evangelicals, Pentecostals, Roman Catholics and members of mainline Protestant churches;[35] the organization claims 2,200,000 members but other sources such as the *People for the American Way* say it has less than 400,000.[36]

The Fairness Doctrine was a policy that required broadcasters to present controversial issues in a fair manner by airing contrasting points of view. The dismantling of the Fairness Doctrine by the Republican-controlled Federal Communications Commission (FCC) in 1987 allowed the religious right and conservative organizations to quickly amass and consolidate media ownership and send a singular focused message to many people at once. This consolidation hindered anyone else's capacity to compete or respond to their statements. Oftentimes, as was demonstrated during the 2004 presidential campaign, one baseless accusation after another was launched before the opponent could respond to the first one. By the time a response was put out by the opponent, the damage to public opinion had been accomplished. The strategy of presenting the right wing Christian and neoconservative agendas leaned on the base feelings [fear], desires [greed] and conceit [hubris] of people. The mood of the country has changed since 1990 such that the public readily accepted the installation of George W. Bush as president even though he did not win the popular vote in the year 2000. In relation to the presidential elections of the year 2000, a company called "Choicepoint, that was found to have ties to the Republican Party, supplied an erroneous voter rolle to the Attorney General of Florida, a Republican, who used it to disenfranchise thousands of African American and other voters which the party knew mostly vote for the Democratic Party. Those votes that were lost would have made the vote in favor of Al Gore even more certain. That same company, Choicepoint, was found to have supplied voter lists to the Mexican government of Mexican voters (against Mexican law) so that that government could disenfranchise them, in order to allow the conservative, pro-business and pro U.S.A. corporations candidate to win the presidential elections. Despite those frauds the U.S.A. population (at least the Democratic Party supporters) did not rise in protest. By contrast, the Mexican voters who supported the Liberal candidate who said he would rescind the NAFTA agreement with the U.S.A. and Canada and make the economy more just for the poor and native American Indian population, did rise up in massive protests.

Other irregularities were also accepted by the U.S.A. population (generally), such as the invasion of Iraq in 2003, and the reelection of George W. Bush in 2004, despite statewide irregularities in the counting of votes and the use of easily hacked electronic voting machines, with no paper trail, supplied by friends of the Bush administration who were known to publicly promise to deliver the state of Ohio to clinch the win of the presidency to Bush.

The Limits of Faith

Published on Thursday, August 28, 2003 by the Cleveland Plain Dealer

Voting Machine Controversy
by Julie Carr Smyth

COLUMBUS - The head of a company vying to sell voting machines in Ohio told Republicans in a recent fund-raising letter that he is "committed to helping Ohio deliver its electoral votes to the president next year."
The Aug. 14 letter from Walden O'Dell, chief executive of Diebold Inc. - who has become active in the re-election effort of President Bush - prompted Democrats this week to question the propriety of allowing O'Dell's company to calculate votes in the 2004 presidential election.

While there have been some writers who presented the duplicitous side of the Republican Party and the neoconservative agenda, it was not until the year 2004 that a counterbalancing force on radio emerged that could challenge the relentless message of the conservative organization. That counterbalancing organization was *Air America Radio.*

Theocracy is not an issue in governmental practice if that is the desire of the people who have that form of government. A more literal term for the exact meaning of "theocracy" is "ecclesiocracy," which denotes rule by a religious leader or body, whereas theocracy would literally mean rule by God.[37] What is at issue is the tyranny imposed by such a government, which can be imposed by any government form. So tyranny is the issue, not theology. In other words, a theocratic government is not necessarily tyrannical. The tyranny comes in when the people are forced to accept traditions they do not want or the government imposes dehumanizing or inhuman punishments for disobeying the theocratic rule. Orthodox, religions that promote faith-based practice, absolutism, literalism and historicity are conducive for religious tyranny because they are designed to demand the conversion of all people within their domain. Thus, it is arrogant for a country to dictate the policies of others if that country purports to be a champion of democracy. It is also hypocritical for such a country to promote the ideal of democracy in other countries while curtailing civil rights or discouraging the practice of religion or encouraging certain religions over others in its own social order.

Grants Flow To Bush Allies On Social Issues
Federal Programs Direct At Least $157 Million By Thomas B. Edsall
Washington Post Staff Writer
Wednesday, March 22, 2006; Page A01

The Limits of Faith

> For years, conservatives have complained about what they saw as the liberal tilt of federal grant money. Taxpayer funds went to abortion rights groups such as Planned Parenthood to promote birth control, and groups closely aligned with the AFL-CIO got Labor Department grants to run worker-training programs.
> In the Bush administration, conservatives are discovering that turnabout is fair play: Millions of dollars in taxpayer funds have flowed to groups that support President Bush's agenda on abortion and other social issues.[38]

What the article does not discuss is the finding that the grants went to religious right organizations and not to religiously center or left organizations. Also, almost all of the money went to conservative Christian organizations and people who support and can vote for the Republican Party, and not to other religions.[39] Therefore, this is mixing religion with politics and a blatant bribery of spiritual culture; it is a corruption of religion itself to pander for votes by appealing to and supporting religious fundamentalists, Pentecostals and dominionists. If the U.S.A. was supposed to be a place for free practice of religion, how would that be possible if the government subsidized one religion over others? If the constitution of the country prevents the country from being controlled by a religion [which would make it an ecclesiocracy], support or discouragement of one form of religion would be clear violation of that principle.

Establishing such a precedent [government financial support of religion] debases religion because it brings it into the arena of corrupt politics. It has been pointed out by some theologians such as Rev. Forrest Church, that the separation of church and state has actually allowed religion to flourish in the United States of America. A similar contention was presented in the book *A New Religious America* by Diana L. Eck. The radicalization of the religious right has reversed that tradition. Furthermore, whenever an industry or area of culture is subsidized, it comes under the control of government, because the subsidized group becomes used to the financial support and develops fear of losing it, so it accedes to the demands of the paying group, the politicians. Thus, it would not be unusual to find religious ministers that promote government policies in order to remain in the good graces of the government. Additionally, conservative preachers have supported political candidates and policies openly or privately, even though that is supposedly against the law.

The Limits of Faith

On February 22, the day of the Michigan state Republican primaries, Christian Coalition Founder Pat Robertson taped a telephone message for a "shadow" campaign in support of Presidential candidate George W. Bush. The message, which went out on phone banks to thousands of Christian Coalition supporters in Michigan, warned that Bush's rival John McCain was against the First Amendment, that he was pro-labor, and that a McCain victory would destroy the Republican Party. Robertson also called McCain's campaign chairman, former New Hampshire Senator Warren Rudman (who is an observant Jew), "a vicious bigot" because Rudman wrote in his 1996 autobiography that the religious right is intolerant. Robertson hoped that his character assassination of Senator McCain would depress voter turnout and swing the closely-contested primary toward Bush, his hand-picked man. But something went wrong. Voter turnout was enormous and McCain carried both Michigan and his home state of Arizona.[40]

On August 22, 2005, Pat Robertson called for the assassination of Venezuelan President Hugo Chavez[41]. However, even though conservative preachers such as Pat Robertson, openly and apparently secretly supported the President and openly spoke out against his opponents, and even advocated assassinating a foreign government leader, they were never prosecuted or at least warned by the justice department for inciting a criminal act, nor contacted by the Internal Revenue Service [I.R.S.] to revoke their status as religious organizations. Yet an anti-war speech [critical of the President] by another pastor did draw that warning. This double standard clearly indicates collusion between the presidential administration and the religious right.

Antiwar Sermon Brings IRS Warning [42]
All Saints Episcopal Church in Pasadena risks losing its tax-exempt status because of a former rector's remarks in 2004. By Patricia Ward Biederman and Jason Felch, Times Staff Writers November 7, 2005

The Internal Revenue Service has warned one of Southern California's largest and most liberal churches that it is at risk of losing its tax-exempt status because of an antiwar sermon two days before the 2004 presidential election. Rector J. Edwin Bacon of All Saints Episcopal Church in Pasadena told many congregants during morning services Sunday that a guest sermon by the church's former rector, the Rev. George F. Regas, on Oct. 31, 2004, had prompted a letter from the IRS.

The Limits of Faith

When religious figures begin to carry on activities that contradict their own religious tenets, and even break laws with impunity, and or operate in collusion with political leaders and outside the law, they have walked into a door that was created by government and religious corruption. The creation of such an alliance in a country that is not supposed to have such alliances signals the condition and direction of the culture towards corruption and dictatorship.

The issue therefore is not whether theocracy is or is not a proper form of government. There have been theocracies in the past. Ancient Egypt existed for thousands of years as a theocracy ["ecclesiocracy"], based on Maat [divine law], administered by the Pharaoh and the priests and priestesses. The Dalai Lama's rule in Tibet, especially before certain twentieth century changes, has been regarded as theocratic type rule. The issue is that in a country where such a form of government is prohibited, where there are many different theological views, such a development will necessarily lead to conflict and abuse of power, repression of less powerful religions and the imposition of orthodox religious views on the rest of the population, that will engender hatred of the domineering religion as well as animosity between religions and the reverse of the stated spiritual goal, to promote peace and closeness to God.

The steady stream of fundamentalist Pentecostalism in the U.S.A. has led to a religious right wing conservative movement that cannot tolerate other religions, other cultures, other points of political view or life in a mixed religious and secular society. The following statements by prominent religious right ministers in the U.S.A. illustrate the hostility and supremacist attitude towards religions other than Christianity, coming from typical leaders of the religious right churches. [highlighted text by Ashby]

> *{Billy} Graham's son not holding back on Islam*[43]
> By Jim Jones -Special to the Star-Telegram
>
> When I heard the Rev. Franklin Graham speak in New Orleans two weeks ago, he focused on proclaiming the saving power of Jesus Christ with only a hint of criticism of Islam.
> <u>"Muhammad didn't die for your sins," he told thousands at the New Orleans Arena. "Buddha didn't die for your sins; Krishna didn't die for your sins. It's Jesus."</u>

The Limits of Faith

But while in New Orleans, Graham again blasted the Muslim faith under the glare of television lights as he told ABC's Nightline that he hasn't changed his mind about Islam, which he called "a very evil and wicked religion" <u>Unlike his father, who never uttered a discouraging word against Islam or any other faith, Franklin Graham has joined Christian broadcaster Pat Robertson, the Rev. Jerry Falwell and others as being among the most outspoken against Islam.</u>
After Sept. 11, 2001, he told NBC News: "We're not attacking Islam, but Islam has attacked us. The God of Islam is not the same God. He's not the Son of God of the Christian or Judeo-Christian faith. <u>It's a different God, and I believe it is a very wicked and evil religion.</u>"

In another program, Franklin Graham also said:

> GRAHAM [video clip]: I've been working in Muslim countries now for, oh, 40 years or more. So I know about Islam. If people think Islam is such a wonderful religion, just go to Saudi Arabia and make it your home. Just live there. If you think Islam is such a wonderful religion, I mean, go and live under the Taliban somewhere.[44]

Rev. Pat Robertson said:

> ROBERTSON [video clip]: These people are crazed fanatics. <u>And I want to say it now. I believe it's motivated by demonic power. It is satanic.</u> And it's time we recognize what we're dealing with.[45]

On the March 17, 2006 Fox News' network opinion program: *The O'Reilly Factor*, the president of the Southern Baptist Theological Seminary, R. Albert Mohler Jr., who also hosts a daily Christian radio show called *The Albert Mohler Program*, agreed with Pat Robertson's [of the *700 Club,*] statements that Muslims are "motivated by demonic power". Mr. Mohler Jr. said:

> MOHLER: Well, I would have to say as a Christian that I believe <u>any belief system, any world view,</u> whether it's Zen Buddhism or Hinduism or dialectical materialism for that matter, Marxism, <u>that keeps persons captive and keeps them from coming to faith in the Lord Jesus Christ, yes, is a demonstration of satanic power</u>...

> And in the case of the two statements from which you pulled there -- from Dr. Graham and from Pat Robertson, they were speaking a deeply Christian truth there that <u>Christians have believed for 2,000 years. And by the way, not with Muslims, because of course now we have only 14 centuries of dealing with the challenge of Islam,</u> **but any**

The Limits of Faith

belief system that keeps persons from coming to Christ we would see as a manifestation of a demonic power.

It would seem that tragedies such as the Sept. 11, 2001 attack on the U.S.A. were an opportunity for religious extremists to more loudly warn about some impending Armageddon. Even before the tragedy, the religious right had engaged in a campaign of fear about the "end times" being near and the need to repent and accept Jesus for salvation. However, the disaster also allowed them to sound the calls of attack on Islamic followers in general, thus allowing them to present to society a supposedly viable threat to Christianity, which is bound up in the "American way of life" that should be preserved at all costs. This form of demagoguery speaks from an arrogant and hubristic perspective, believing that Christianity is the only true religion and therefore those who follow it are entitled to survive and all others should die if necessary, because they are all following false religions and are going to hell anyway [for not believing in and being saved by Jesus]. It is also a fear-based argument that finds many ears and many who agree and support it. The summons to fear and the dilemma of what course of action to take was answered by them not as a call to arms against sin and corruption, and to reflection and peacemaking, but to hate those who are different, as well as a call against other religions, and Islam in particular. It is also a call against secularism, and even other forms of Christianity that are not as "zealous." Those people who are unsure of themselves are often caught up in the fervor of the sure sounding words of the religious right preachers or they may acquiesce out of guilt or simple honest faith in their words. In that way, the religious far right has gained for itself great power and influence in U.S.A. culture, even though it remains a minority, making up perhaps less than 30% of the population, but with some of the loudest voices among the clergy. Nevertheless, this minority would sacrifice all democratic values in order to force the rest of the country to follow their narrow system of belief.

The ideals of manifest destiny and exeptionalism of the United States, as a superpower, are very much inline with the Judeo-Christian tradition of the special nature and special covenant of the Jews, and therefore the Christians, with God, because the culture of the United States was founded on secular and Western Judea-Christian principles.[46] These are ideas that contribute to the notion of superiority over all other religions, and cultures, just as the early Jews assigned to themselves, by means of the dictum from God, the superiority over all other religions. That dictum was and continues to be the entitlement of and mission to conquer the land of Canaan.[47] Only, now for the United States, the land of Canaan, the "promised land," is not just the Middle East, but also the entire world.[48] So the roots of the superpower mentality and its causes can be traced to deep-rooted delusions and romanticized ideas, desires and dreams, as well as meteorological issues that will be explained later.

The Judeo-Christian religion, as it was practiced in Europe, has constituted an extreme dogmatic materialistic approach to spirituality and religious practice. It contributes immensely to the Superpower syndrome and its mental complexes that lead to conflict. The Judeo-Christian religion's material culture and reliance on the phenomenology of existence as opposed to the interconnectedness of life and the transcendental nature of human evolution have contributed to the rigidity in the superpower culture with the concomitant disdain for what is not empirical, quantifiable or measurable. Consequently, the religions, values and ideas of other cultures are rejected, in favor of Western science and Western values, and hence Western hegemony becomes the legitimate social imperative and governmental guiding principle.

The religious right [fundamentalists and extremists] supported by acquiescent moderate Christians and the secular populations [by their general support of the government] have attained unprecedented influence in the government upon which they stress the apocalyptic fear of the "end times." That is partly accomplished by citing proposed meanings to Bible prophecies that supposedly speak of Russia leading a coalition of Arabs to destroy Israel[49] and other doomsday scenarios that will trigger events that will lead to Armageddon. Some Christian groups openly advocate using U.S.A. military power to attack all who oppose the U.S.A. to avoid Armageddon. Others advocate such attacks on Arab countries in order to trigger them and bring forth the destruction of civilization to bring about the apocalypse, which is part of a stream of religious thought within Christianity almost from its inception. However, that segment of Christians has been claiming unsuccessfully that the end is near for over 1500 years.

The Limits of Faith

In the late 20th century, the religious right seized upon two issues they could use to incite the ire of ordinary "god fearing" religious people in order to motivate them to get involved with politics and go to cast votes. The two issues were abortion, and homosexual rights. Religious right adherents were motivated against abortion and homosexuality by convincing them these were cataclysmic sins that were dragging the country's morals down and further, that were supported by the Democratic Party. Therefore, they were motivated out of fear. It is ironic that there are so many other sins mentioned in the bible that are not used to gain such an advantage, like adultery, that if were treated the same way would devastate the leadership of the religious right, and republican and democratic parties and expose them as hypocrites. The factor of the selective choice of those sins to be concentrated upon and not others, and the fact that other sins are mentioned more in the bible, but are not mentioned by the religious right leaders reveals a certain double standard, and thus also a particular political agenda. Those two issues were used successfully by religious leaders who aligned themselves with the Republican Party in order to give that party an edge in the electoral process. Those same voters tended to be conservatives and supported the candidates who seemed to be supporting the religious right agenda. However, though the Republican Party has actually acted in support of the religious right, there is overwhelming support for the corporations and the corporate agenda. In a way, the cause of the corporations was merged with that of the religious right, thus making capitalism and Republican Party affiliation an almost religious duty. Thus, even though the association with the religious right offers a kind of moral veneer to the republican neoconservative and corporate agenda, it remains an unjust and immoral schema for controlling the culture and profiting to the utmost from the labor of ordinary citizens as well as the slave labor of citizens of other countries.

The Limits of Faith

Passover and The Danger of Religious Hegemony and Religious Absentmindedness

Passover is an example of how some religious traditions from some cultures take on realism and can affect other cultures negatively. In recent years there have been many Jewish groups that have been trying to share the Passover ritual with peoples outside the Jewish community. This may a commendable goal in principle but there are some issues that arise out of this effort that may not have been considered.

Passover is an important Jewish festival commemorating the supposed exodus of the Israelites from Egypt and their safe flight across the Red Sea. This flight, described in the Book of Exodus of the Judeo-Christian Bible, was led by Moses. The name of the festival (Hebrew pesah, "passing over" or "protection") is derived from the instructions given to Moses by God (see Exodus 12:3-17). In order to encourage the Egyptians to allow the Israelites to leave Egypt, God intends to "smite all the first-born ... both man and beast" in the land. To protect themselves, the Israelites were told to mark their dwellings with lamb's blood so that God can identify and thus "pass over" them.

The celebration of the holiday begins after sundown on the 14th day of Nisan, the first month of the Jewish ecclesiastical year, about the time of the vernal equinox. In accordance with rabbinic law, Jews living outside the limits of ancient Palestine celebrate the holiday for eight days and partake of a ceremonial meal, known as the Seder, on the first two nights. The Seder consists of prescribed foods, each of which symbolizes some aspect of the ordeal undergone by the Israelites during their supposed enslavement in Egypt.

Exodus is the second book of the Old Testament of the Christian Bible. It was named Exodus because it relates the departure or escape of the

The Limits of Faith

Israelites from Egypt and their wanderings through the desert up to Mount Sinai. Exodus supposedly records the events between the death in Egypt of Joseph, the favorite son of the Hebrew patriarch Jacob, and the erection by the Israelites of the Tabernacle at Sinai. The first 15 chapters supposedly tell of the oppression of the Israelites by the Egyptians after Joseph's death, of the birth and preservation of Moses from slaughter, of God's selection of Moses to lead the children of Israel out of Egypt, of the ten plagues inflicted on the Egyptians, and of God's deliverance of the Israelites both from the land of Egypt and from the Egyptian army at the Red Sea.

Both the existence of the Jews in ancient times as well as the occurrence of the Passover are items of speculation since there is no independent evidences to support them. According to the Encarta Encyclopedia while the book of Exodus is traditionally ascribed to Moses, it is believed by most modern scholars to have been compiled in its present form by members of the Jewish priesthood around 550 BC.[50] Certain parts of the book (for example, chap. 25-31), in which God describes to Moses the manner in which the Tabernacle and its furnishings are to be built, and the dress and ritual of the priests, are thought to date from earlier times and from other traditions. For example, the story of Moses, being found by the queen after floating in a basket down a river occurs before the time of Abraham, in Mesopotamia. The section containing the code of religious and civil ordinances (20:23-23:33) is of even greater antiquity and may possibly have originated in pre-Mosaic times. We have seen and it is accepted by many scholars, that the Jewish teachings are in part derived from preexisting Ancient Egyptian wisdom texts. (Ex. THE TEACHINGS OF THE BIBLE PROVERBS XXII. 17-XXIII. 14; correlate to THE TEACHINGS OF AMENEMOPE of Ancient Egypt.[51]

The Limits of Faith

From Wikipedia Encyclopedia:

> As far as archeologists can tell, neighboring countries that kept many written records, such as Egypt and Assyria, have no writings about the stories of the Bible or its main characters before 650 BCE.
>
> The historicity of the Exodus of the Israelites from Egypt is a matter of some speculation. Looking for hints in the extensive Egyptian records, some scholars identify the Israelites with the Hyksos, Asian tribes that inhabited Egypt in the 17-16 centuries BCE. Others suggested the Apir which are reminded occasionally between the 15th and 11th centuries BCE. The earliest known reference to "Israel" (c 1200BCE), is the "Victory Stele" (or "Merneptah Stele", referred to erroneously as the "Israel Stele") of the Egyptian pharaoh Merneptah, in which among other victories it is recorded that "Israel is laid waste; his seed is not". Egypt continued to rule the area until the 10th century BCE.

Present day scholars ascribe the date of the present version of the Old Testament of the Jewish Bible (5 books of Moses) to be 550 B.C.E. This means that this is the time when the version was formed, that is putting together legends and varying strands of philosophical thought that later came to represent so called Jewish theology, ritual and myth. So if the Jewish Bible is recounting events that were supposed to have occurred over 500 years earlier (before 1000 BCE), where is the evidence in the form of archeological confirmation, architecture or remnant of those original scriptures? In essence it is similar to the case of early Christianity, where there are no records of any particular person called "Jesus" until 1-2 generations after Jesus supposedly lived (end of the first century A.C.E. (62-95 A.C.E.)). There are no independent records, outside of the Judeo-Christian Bible, of an Exodus, Moses, the killing of the first born or of plagues in Egypt, parting of seas, etc., just as there is no record of Jesus' miracles in the times they are ascribed. The period of the creation of the Jewish Bible coincides with the adoption or synthesis of preexisting myths or fabrications of new concepts in Jewish theology. The concept of an end time battle between good and evil that ends the world is a preexisting Zoroastrian concept. A prominent example of cooptation and synthesis of previously existing theological concepts is the emergence of the "devil" in Judaism. Prior to that point in time, Satan meant "an opponent" and not a particular devil being with actual existence. At around the 6th century B.C.E., Satan appears in the Old Testament as an individual angel who is subordinate to God. Gradually, as Jewish and Christian tradition developed around this idea, Satan became known as a personality who was the source of all evil, and was responsible for leading human beings into sin, a concept that was not in Ancient Egyptian Religion. In later Jewish tradition, and therefore also in early Christian thought, this title became a proper name. Satan was then seen as a personified adversary, not only of human beings, but also primarily of God.

The only possible archeological record of the Jewish people in relation to Ancient Egypt is contained in the Merneptah Stele (Victory Stele" (or "Merneptah Stele", referred to erroneously as the "Israel Stele")). The Stele is a commemoration to Pharaoh Merneptah's (son of Rameses II) raid in Canaan, during the fifth year of his rule (ca. 1207 B.C.). It contains a listing of the people that were conquered in the land of Canaan (Palestine, area wherein the modern state of Israel is presently located.) There is a particular name of a people which is translated below:

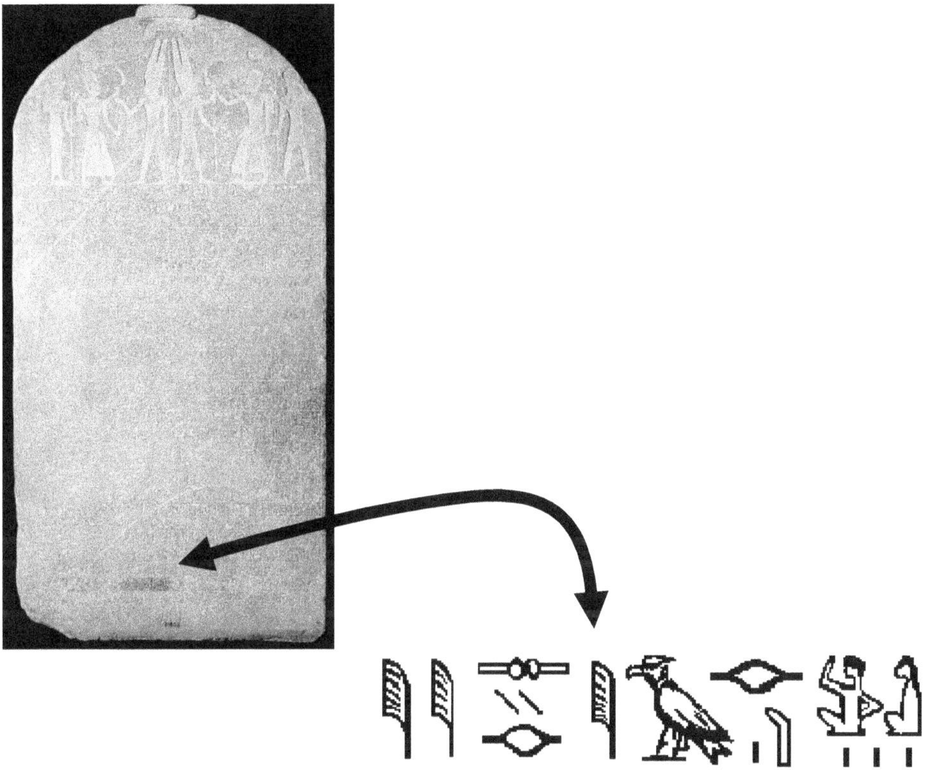

The Limits of Faith

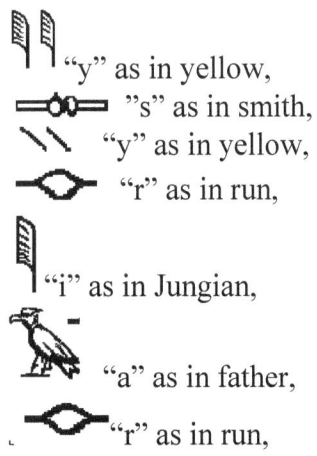

Ysyriar + symbol: "foreigner" and symbol "people"

"y" as in yellow,
"s" as in smith,
"y" as in yellow,
"r" as in run,
"i" as in Jungian,
"a" as in father,
"r" as in run,

determinative: foreigner,

determinative meaning "people" (men and women)

The Limits of Faith

Some scholars,[52] after linguistic analyses of the designation Israel in the Merneptah Stele find that the Egyptian designation is properly translated as Israel. This author (Ashby) agrees that this term Ysyriar used in the stele can be translated as "Israel." Nevertheless, it seems reasonable to ascribe this term to, as the stele relates, peoples who lived in Asia Minor (Canaan) and went under the name Ysyriar as written in Ancient Egyptian language (Medu Neter). While the circumstantial evidence of the similarity of the names Ysyriar and Israel, and the fact that they are described as living in Canaan as the Jews of the Bible suggests that it could be the same people, other scholars have pointed out (and this author agrees) that there is no way to tell if the term relates to the Jews of the Bible since the determinatives used to describe the Ysyriar designate them as foreign peoples and not as the other conquered groups which are described as nations, that is people with a geographical location, implying a physical domain such as a kingdom. If it was the Israelites of the Bible there was no land of the Israelites, no Jerusalem and no State of Israel at that time. This means that the Ysyriar is perhaps as a socio-ethnic entity "outside" of Egypt and under the control of Egypt. So therefore, if they are the Jews of the Bible they are not in Egypt and if they left Egypt in some Exodus previously, then at this time they would be subject peoples. In any case this designation does not agree with the Jewish-Christian Bible when it says that the Jews were freed from the Egyptians and that the Egyptian God defeated Pharaoh and the army of the Egyptians. In fact this stele points to the reverse; if it is to be ascribed to the people we refer to as Jews then it is a contradiction of the account of the Bible because the Israelites would be described as subject peoples under the control of Egypt. On the other hand, the term Hebrew is an even better correlation. The term Hebrew means "A member of or descendant from one of a group of northern Semitic peoples including the Israelites."[53] The Hebrews were nomadic peoples in and around Canaan and the Israelites were one group of those Hebrews who used the Hebrew language. But there were Hebrews who did not follow the Jewish religion and become part of the Israeli ethnic group. But recall that according to the Bible the Israelites originated with Abraham who was from Ur of the Chaldees. He went into Egypt with his family and then later the people following the Jewish religion supposedly emerged from Egypt and only then settled in Palestine, the area that they later established themselves and made their holy city and temple (Jerusalem).

The Limits of Faith

Thus, it is impossible for the Jews of the Bible to have met with Rameses the Great as is intimated in Jewish tradition, because he existed over 700 years before the creation of the Old Testament. If the creators of the Old Testament are referring to the Pharaoh it is because he was, as other legendary figures, the most powerful image in Ancient Egyptian history whose legend rolled down through history as a model for all Pharaohs who came after. Consequently he was the best target to confront in the story of Exodus. In this way the Jews confronted and defeated the Pharaoh, the most powerful person on earth, and they also defeated the gods of the Egyptians, who were recognized as the most powerful of all in the ancient world and the Jewish priesthood gained the admiration and prestige to control their people. So like a prize fighter in boxing or a gunslinger in the old west, when the young gun kills the old he takes the reputation of the old; so too the Jews sought to take the prestige and reputation of Ancient Egyptian Religion. The same procedure was followed by the Upanishadic priests of early Hinduism, who supplanted the gods of the Vedic age by showing how the Upanishadic era divinities that came after were stronger.

The use of myth to elevate one spiritual tradition over another was used before the Jewish tradition advanced the notion that the Jewish God had supplanted the Ancient Egyptian Gods. In India, the emergence of Hinduism saw a similar situation as with the one that occurred between the Jewish and Ancient Egyptian Religion. Around the same period (c. 800 B.C.E.-600 B.C.E.), the earlier Vedic-Aryan religious teachings related to the God Indra (c. 1,000 B.C.E.) were supplanted by the teachings related to the Upanishadic and Vaishnava tradition. The Vaishnava tradition includes the worship of the god Vishnu, as well as his avatars (divine incarnations), in the form of Rama and Krishna. The Vaishnava tradition was developed by the indigenous Indian peoples to counter, surpass and evolve beyond the Vedic religious teachings. In the epic stories known as the Ramayana and the Mahabharata[54], Vishnu incarnates as Rama and Krishna, respectively, and throughout these and other stories it is related how Vishnu's incarnations are more powerful than Indra's, who is portrayed as being feeble and weak. Some of the writings of the Upanishadic Tradition,[55] the writings which succeed the Vedic tradition, contain specific verses which seem to profess that the wisdom of the Vedas is lesser than that of the Upanishads, and that they therefore supersede the Vedas. One such statement can be found in the *Mundaka Upanishad*. The following segment details the view of the two sets of scriptures in relation to each other and the two forms of knowledge. (italicized portions are by Ashby)

> Those who know Brahman (God)... say that there are two kinds of knowledge, the higher and the lower. *The lower is knowledge of the Vedas* (the Rik, the Sama, the Yajur, and the Atharva), and also of phonetics, grammar, etymology, meter, and astronomy. *The higher is the knowledge of that by which one knows the changeless reality.*

There are no records of the Jews in Ancient Egypt as slaves in the form described in the Bible. The misrepresentation about the Jews having been the slave laborers who created the Great Pyramids has been soundly debunked in the last 15 years by archeological discoveries of the true laborers, the Ancient Egyptian people themselves. The debunking was so complete that the mayor of New York, Ed Kotch, who previously contributed to the spreading of that fable, publicly apologized and reversed himself. However, the Jews are mentioned in Ancient Egypt as subjects of the Egyptian empire as were many other peoples who paid tribute to Egypt. In any case, the Bible itself states that the Jewish people went into Egypt voluntarily seeking refuge not once but twice, under the leadership of Abraham (Genesis 12-17) and again under the leadership of Joseph (Genesis 47). Later, Joseph (father of Jesus), Mary and baby Jesus sought refuge in Egypt also (Matthew - Chap. 2). It is interesting that Egypt is so maligned in the Bible, yet it is the source of much Jewish theology and the cause of the existence of the Jewish and Christian religions, for they would not have survived without Egypt.

> "What is now called the Christian religion has existed among the Ancients and was not absent from the beginning of the human race until Christ came in the flesh from which time the true religion which was already in existence began to be called Christian."
> -St. Augustine

The events in Ancient Egypt leading up to the sixth century B.C.E. (600 BCE-500 BCE) and afterwards read like an ever increasing society in chaos and civilization in decline due to invasions from Asia. Unrest, wars and the breakdown in social order prompted a migration out of Egypt over the period from the sixth century B.C.E. to the Islamic invasion and conquest period (642-1517 A.C.E.).

The Limits of Faith

In the Late Period of Ancient Egyptian history the Persians conquered Egypt and ruled between 525 B.C.E. and 404 B.C.E. This event and the ensuing events led to a highly unstable social structure and displacements of Ancient Egyptian people through slavery and forced labor. At that time there were no Pharaohs named Rameses. The last Rameses Pharaoh ruled before 1000 B.C.E. so if a group of Ancient Egyptians wanted to leave during that time and form a new religion they might have done so in the midst of war and chaos, not through a confrontation with a powerful Pharaoh as is recounted dramatically in the Bible. Note that if 600,000 people comprised the numbers of Jews who left Egypt that would have been a substantial portion of the population and that more than anything else would have caused a major disruption in Egyptian society. Yet there is no record of such a disruption.

One of the most important events of the 6th century B.C.E. which influenced the rest of the ancient world was the first Persian conquest of Egypt in the sixth century B.C.E. When Cambyses II reigned (529-522 BC) as king of Persia, he conquered Egypt and proved to be a despotic ruler. According to Herodotus, Cambyses II was a dissolute and inhuman despot, prone to drunken or insane rages in which he committed sacrilegious and cruel acts.[56] Egypt was captured by Alexander the Great and then the Romans. Yet, the Jews settled in Alexandria (northern Egypt and capital of the Greek occupiers of Egypt). There they created the *Septuagint*. The Septuagint is the name given to the ancient Greek translation of the Hebrew scriptures of Judaism as they existed at the time. Before this time the books which today constitute the Old Testament had not been compiled. Previously, the Jewish leaders had been debating for hundreds of years as to which books should be included as canonical Jewish texts and they found fertile spiritual teachings, as Alexandria was a hub of cultures at that time. Here once again Alexandria, Egypt and the mystical philosophy of Ancient Egyptian Religion and its derivative, Gnosticism, played an important part in the consolidation of Jewish theology. The term "diabolos" was used for the *Septuagint* or Greek translation of the Jewish Bible, not referring to human beings, but in order to translate the Hebrew word *ha-satan* (the satan).

In closing, Passover is a Jewish ritual that is meant to sustain the mythic event of a Jewish exodus from Ancient Egypt. It did not happen historically but its purpose as a story has political significance to the Jews.

The Limits of Faith

It portrays Jews as martyrs, as underdogs, and sets up the justification for murder and dispossession of other peoples lands (Exodus 33 1-2). It is also meant to sustain the cohesion of Jewish practitioners through a common story or history of faith. It is also a means to promote the idea of the powerful Jewish God defeating the Egyptians and their God so as to elevate Judaism to prominence, it having a God who actually defeated the most powerful nation of the ancient world, as a supposed "historical fact," unlike other religions which just supposedly have only empty myths. It is simply another misconception that is to be debunked so that the record may be viewed correctly. The 6th century saw the emergence of many spiritual traditions and Judaism can be added to the list of all those who drank from the waters of the Nile and blossomed forth with spiritual teaching, albeit flawed, not following the original tradition.

However, the lesson should be learned that one people do not have to usurp the traditions of others or denigrate the traditions of others in order to bring forth their own, unless their own culture or religion is weak, erroneous or fanatical. Why was it necessary for the Jews and Christians to close down the Egyptian temples and other religions of the ancient world by force? Because ordinary people did not want to follow those teachings of the Jews and Christians, which were considered new bizarre cults. So the Jews and Christians used violence to close all other religions and force-converted their followers just as the Muslims did later. Violence against others, denigration of the culture and religion of others, suppression of others, cooptation of the teachings and symbols of others, forced conversion of others, etc. are factors that let us know of sources of the flaws in religions that survive to this day. Consider the present day Catholic Church. Pope John Paul II said that Buddhism is a bad religion. Now with the new pope we discover that he was the intellectual force behind John Paul II and has written that Christianity is the only true religion! Proponents of Islam are even more dogmatic. In the absence of contrary voices, the misconceptions, demagoguery and outright falsehoods become real in the minds of most people especially after hundreds of years of repetition and lack of critical thinking. If ther is a question about why the Ancient Egyptian Temple system persisted through the Persian conquest, the Assyrian conquest, the Greek conquest, and the Roman conquest, but came to a close during the emergence of the Roman Catholic Church, they have no further to look than the following statement by one of the leaders of the early church. The reputed founder of Christian-

Egyptian monasticism, Saint Anthony, led his followers in active attacks against the Ancient Egyptian Temples which practiced the ancient Egyptian religion. The ignorance, intolerance and denigration of the Kamitan Temples and their images are readily evident in the following quote by Saint Anthony.

> *"Which is better, to confess the cross or to attribute adulteries and pederastys to these so called gods, beasts, reptiles and the images of men? The Christians, by their faith in God prove that the demons whom the Egyptians consider gods are no gods! The Christians trample them underfoot and drive them out for what they are, deceivers and corruptors of men. Through Jesus-Christ our lord, Amen"*

Let us understand clearly the history, politics and social conditions of religious practice during the time of the creation of the Jewish and Christian religions. Judaism and Christianity were born in an era of degraded Greek culture and debauched Roman society. Orthodox, dogmatic, and fanatical religions are responses to degraded politics and extreme human suffering, such as was perpetrated by the Asiatics of Asia Minor, the Greeks and the Romans through unceasing wars of conquest. Orthodox religion is easy to impose when people's liberty to practice other religions is limited and when people are suffering greatly and are in fear. They will listen to demagogs and follow the behests of dictators even unto their own death. That is why it is important to point out the histories that are overlooked so that all traditions may have equal chance to express their teachings and not supplant others through erroneous histories.

Passover-Part 2

The Passover celebration of the Jews is certainly based on an unproven idea but through the generations it has become an established dogma as many other rituals, to support a certain belief system, a certain heritage, culture and history. Due to ignorance certain African Americans, who may be well meaning, seek to find friendship, belonging, camaraderie, etc. through intercultural associations.

The Limits of Faith

On April 22nd, 2005 a film segment called *Freedom Seder* aired on a program called *Religion and Ethics Newsweekly* (Episode no. 834 - *Freedom Seder*). It attempted to show how some followers of Jewish religion were trying to share the Jewish tradition with African Americans and others to promote peace and understanding. An irony in that effort might be that if the Bible is to be taken as the true ancient history of Judaism the original Jews were "black" Africans, Egyptians who were enslaved by their rulers of Egypt who were also "black" Africans since it has been demonstrated that the Ancient Egyptians were "black Africans like the Nubians (present day Sudanese).[57] In ancient times there were no "white Jews" or European Jews. But in recent times some Jews, along with Christians, helped to enslave Africans in the European and American slave trade and now they are celebrating their supposed freedom with those whom they also enslaved and who enslaved them in the past? Further irony is that the African Americans are, in participating with this ritual, actually saying that they agree with the Jewish take on history and that they were the enslavers of the Jews since the Ancient Egyptians were "black." They are also validating the Jewish wrongs against the African American community. It is in many ways a convoluted and problematical history that has left the minds of most people confused. But that confusion occurs due to misinformation, forgetfulness (absentmindedness) and lack of reflection.

One of the important things for us to understand in regard to the Jewish – African American relationship or any relationship between cultures is that there are varied levels of socio-political-economic interests that are working beneath the surface. Firstly, as scholars such as Leonard Jeffries have pointed out, there were Christians and Jews involved in the African slave trade. That is a deplorable aspect of the cultural relationship in itself. However, throughout USA history Jews have sought to ally with the "negro" struggle for liberation at certain times.

Note that when we speak of "Jews" we are referring to a group of people who identify themselves as followers of a particular religion called "Judaism." Jews are not a particular race group. (*The term Jew is really an abbreviation of the term Judah, for the Southern Kingdom*) The religion of certain people who were Hebrew (Canaanite nomads) came to be known as Judaism. Judaism is not just a religion but a socio-political-economic association with the agenda of accumulating wealth for the Jewish population.

It is natural to seek the wellbeing of oneself and one's people but it can be an aggression towards others when it is at the expense of others, the hoarding of wealth and power that deprives others and keeps them in economic destitution and political subjugation. In reality, the conspiracy to provide for one's own wellbeing alone eventually leads to partisanship, greed and animosity towards others and from others. The true way to peace and prosperity is a conspiracy to promote that everyone (all groups, all religions, all ethnicities) is assured of having the basic necessities of life and opportunities to prosper and evolve and that the rights of all are protected. Note that not all people who follow Judaism, Christianity or Islam hold the view of politically, religiously or economically dominating other populations. However, the masses those groups generally benefit from the economic domination strategy initiated by the minority unless they publicly repudiate it and take no part in benefiting from it. We must realize we are all interconnected as one humanity and if there is injustice in any segment of humanity that will negatively impact on the rest of humanity at some point in time.

Truly righteous people do not subscribe to moral relativism, applying morality when it suits them but not when it concerns the welfare of others. Moral relativism reveals the character flaws of a human being or even a culture. Nevertheless, that flaw in many Jewish communities throughout history has led to animosity towards the Jews and sometimes even the destruction of their property, the usurpation of their wealth or even the killing of their populations. In all cultures there are those who seek to promote righteousness and fairness and equal distribution of natural resources. After all POLITICS is supposed to be the negotiation of people for the distribution of resources. When a group gains too much power (in the form of material success and technological advancement) and is taken over by the greedy, the despotic, the demagogs, and when the people become ignorant, greedy and selfish, the degradation of society and the wars of conquest to subjugate others and steal their wealth are not far behind. Nowadays the robbery occurs through propping up despotic governments (neocolonialism: coercion and control of local compliant native rulers), usury loans through world banks, slave labor wages and when those means fail, an army can be sent in under any pretext, such as ridding the world of a bad regime or eradicating weapons of mass destruction, etc.

Throughout history religion has been used by those in power, the demagogs, the aristocracy, and the oligarchy, to stir up fervor, to incite the populace to actions that support the true agenda as dictated by the real religion of those who control society. That religion is the religion of greed and that is driven by fear and sustained with power and power is sustained by technology and technology costs money. They are fearful of losing control and losing the pleasure of status and power. The fear of losing control supersedes the natural decency of human ethics. It may not appear so but religious strife, social strife (even racism) and economic strife are all due to greed and greed is caused by ignorance; ignorance of the true essence of the self.

Human beings are not inherently evil, nor is one group more intelligent than another. The debate over the influence of genes or the environment has occupied much reflection from scientists throughout history. The issue should be thought of in the following context: Genes do not fix behavior. Rather, they establish a range of possible reactions to a range of possible experiences that the environment can provide. The soul comes to the world with its genes (unconscious impressions from previous lives). Then while interacting in the body and its genes, the souls experience a range of situations. But they are bound by certain parameters of culture, world history, social interactions, etc. In that maelstrom they somehow evolve though suffering in the pursuit of happiness until the time of death and future rebirth to begin the cycle again, that is, unless the cycle is broken and enlightenment is pursued. Those who reject the constriction of spiritual genes and DNA will break the cycle. Those who subscribe to the idea of finite human existence and the "survival of the fittest," as well as the idea of race, will fall prey to the mellay of life. Some groups have a propensity towards certain characteristics if those features are cultivated and elicited in them, but they are not endemic nor are they insurmountable. Even such devastating social scourges as racism are redeemable.

If a person wants to believe that racism is the cause of western aggression, they need to answer where was racism before 500 years ago? Before slavery in the Americas, Africans and Europeans interacted, traded and commingled since ancient times, so there was no history of racism as we know it today in ancient times. In the beginning of the USA colonies, whites and blacks were enslaved together and actually there were more European slaves and indentured servants than Africans but when it became possible to produce fantastic profits by enslaving Africans the rationale was created that degraded Africans and now we are still dealing with that legacy. The point is that the imperative for racism and slavery, as well as the viciousness and violence towards Africans originated with the greed and power impetus and that racism is a ploy to achieve wealth and power. Racism, either as a psychological attitude in "white" people o people of European descent or as a socio-political-economic system of enslaving Africans was not there in the beginning of the USA so it is a false cause for the mistreatment of Africans. Racism is a philosophy that was developed to rationalize and explain the enslavement of human beings based on the color of their skin. It naturally degraded into a form of torture and debasement of Africans due to the propensity towards depravity and amorality that is contained in the capacity of people who have developed in western culture towards technological advancement, and capitalist ideations, as well as the fear of violence (European society has experienced much more violence than other cultures, from the Roman subjugation to the almost annual invading hoards from Gaul, Hungary (Huns), the Vandals, the Vikings, etc. (barbarians).

Religious demagoguery is another form of ploy to use religion to achieve the same ends (wealth and power). Demagogs use fanaticism to whip up the feelings of the ignorant populace into an emotional frenzy. It was used by Constantine and Theodosius to consolidate the declining social order of the Roman Empire. It was used by Charlemagne to consolidate the remnants of the Roman culture after it had fallen to create a viable European culture and resist the invading Arab-Muslims and invading hoards of barbarians. It was used by Muhammad and his followers to conquer Asia Minor and North Africa. It was used by the Jews to conquer the lands of Canaan. The Crusades were not about liberating the "holy lands" but rather about sacking and looting the lands of the "infidels" to enrich the aristocracy of Europe. And the list goes on…Now we see it again in our day, with preemptive wars of conquest for oil, the present day source of wealth and power. Many people do not know that during the oil "crisis" of the 1970's when Saudi Arabia placed an oil embargo on the USA, plans and preparations were under way to invade Saudi Arabia, so it

The Limits of Faith

is no surprise that many political analysts see the USA is friendliness with Israel as not about religious solidarity between Christians and Jews but it is a foothold in the Middle East. Prior to the 20th century there was no interest in the Middle East or in assisting Jews to acquire a homeland, but when the industrial countries discovered oil reserves there they rushed to colonize the area; first among these were the British empire and the USA. Iraq had to be attacked not because it posed a threat of weapons but a threat of reduced USA control over its oil. And now notice the timing of the attempts by the USA to reconcile with Jews and support the Jewish state (late 1960s) that coincides with the new economic interest of the 20th century (oil). After centuries of anti-Semitism the USA government has thrown its support behind a Jewish state, allowing the Israelis to develop nuclear weapons, create Bantustans, or reservations for Palestinians - appropriating their land, (as the USA government did to the Native Americans-stealing their land), etc.

Many people do not know that the Catholic Church is one source of the anti-semitism problems that Jews have faced throughout history. Forty years ago (1965), the Catholic Church meeting called Vatican II officially abandoned the Church's teaching that the Jews were responsible for the death of Jesus Christ. The recent movie by Mel Gibson stirred up this issue again by simply presenting dialog that is directly based on the verses in the gospel of the Christian Bible. (Some examples are below) Consider the danger of scriptures that can be misconstrued or taken out of contexts. Ironically, according to the Bible the Jews were indeed responsible for Jesus' death but that does not mean that all Jews should be killed because of that or should be made to suffer for all time; just as whites should not be responsible for the atrocities of their ancestors who enslaved Africans- UNLESS they do not acknowledge the wrongdoing of their ancestors and seek forgiveness for it, and if they do not stop benefiting from the wrongdoing and do not make restitution. Actually, the Bible says that that is exactly what should happen (see **Matthew 27:25)**. Ironically, the same Jewish Bible (Torah) that allowed Christians to create an anti-Semitic movement that played into the hands of Hitler (a Catholic) and allowed him to justify exterminating Jews, also played into the hands of American slave-owners who cited the biblical story of Ham to show that black Africans should be enslaved by God's decree. So the Jews have suffered much due to their own fault (according to the Bible) in creating such scriptures that set them apart from other peoples. The Christian resentment about the death of Jesus at the hands of the Jews visited upon the Jews sufferings as their own scriptures led to the sufferings of Africans. There are many such flaws in the Jewish, Christian and Islamic bibles. Hardly can one find any such kinds of statements in the bibles of non-western religions. The anti-Semitic statements of the Bible played into the hands of those who wanted to stir up strife against Jews and drive them out of their businesses and homes so that they could taken over; all the while many times it was the masses at the behest of demagogs, racists and dictators that did the actual dirty work of riots, lynching, and other atrocities.

Below there are presented some biblical statements supporting the idea that the Jews were responsible for Jesus' Death that were used to create anti-semitic fervor and violence against Jews:

> **Mark 11:18** "And the scribes and chief priests heard *it,* and sought how they might destroy him: for they feared him, because all the people was astonished at his doctrine."

> **John 5:16-18** "And therefore did the Jews persecute Jesus, and sought to slay him, because he had done these things on the sabbath day. *17* But Jesus answered them, My Father worketh hitherto, and I work. *18* Therefore the Jews sought the more to kill him, because he not only had broken the sabbath, but said also that God was his Father, making himself equal with God." The Jews conspired to put Jesus to death!

> **John 11:47-53** *53* Then from that day forth they took counsel together for to put him to death."

> **Matthew 27:22-25** "Pilate saith unto them, What shall I do then with Jesus which is called Christ? *They* all say unto him, Let him be crucified. *23* And the governor said, Why, what evil hath he done? But they cried out the more, saying, Let him be crucified. *24* When Pilate saw that he could prevail nothing, but *that* rather a tumult was made, he took water, and washed *his* hands before the multitude, saying, I am innocent of the blood of this just person: see ye *to it. 25* Then answered all the people, and said, His blood *be* on us, and on our children."

In an ABCNEWS *Primetime* poll (Feb. 16, 2004), Six in 10 people said the Biblical accounts of Moses parting the Red Sea, God creating the world in six days and Noah and the flood happened that way, word for word. Evangelical Protestants are even more apt to hold this view; about nine in 10 of them take these accounts literally. If the Bible is to be believed literally as most Christians often ascertain, why was Mel Gibson's film (*The Passion of the Christ*) forced to cut certain most offensive portions of the movie to please the Jewish community? What does it mean that he took that action but the statements of the Bible were not repudiated, revised or changed? That cannot be done because it (Bible) is touted as the "word of God," the absolute truth. Is it any wonder why the western religions are in strife and its followers are easily mentally disturbed? Is there any wonder why across the board, one-quarter of Americans or more — evangelical and non-evangelical Protestants, Catholics and others — accept the notion that all Jews today bear responsibility for the death of Jesus and why so many people still believe that Africans should be slaves and that they are inferior to whites?

Literalism and the imposition of historicity on Judaism and Christianity may promote more converts and adherents in an environment of social strife because the argument about the veracity and urgency of those religions may appear more forceful. However, those adherents who adopt such philosophies under those kinds of conditions may not be critical thinkers because if they were they would not get past the contradictions which nullify the claims.

Some present day Jewish and Christian authors complain that people are too bent on proving everything of the Bible. It is an argument that reasons like "absence of evidence of Israel in Ancient Egypt is proof that the Bible is true." Firstly, the search for concrete evidence is elicited by those leaders of Judaism and Christianity who say that the Bible presents "historical events." Secondly, the burden of proof of anything is on the person who makes an assertion, not on the one who does not assert. In this essay I am asserting and demonstrating simply that there is no evidence to support that a Passover ever occurred and that the Jewish religion developed out of Ancient Egyptian religion. Those who assert that the Bible is true have the responsibility to prove it. It is not our responsibility to disprove their assertions. It is not irrational to make an assertion, like proposing a theory, but it is irrational to ascertain that a theory is true without presenting any corroborating evidence. In this case the Bible is the theory and there is not historical, archeological, biological, etc., evidence

The Limits of Faith

to support it. This is a common rhetorical technique to obfuscate a point in discussion or debate in western culture. In reality there can be no debate because there is nothing to debate. However, engaging others in a debate creates the quandary in people's minds, such as "maybe it could be true." Yet there is no debate and but nevertheless a large part of the world is gripped by the conflict caused by those who follow this delusion. Many Jews and Christians want to have it both ways, that the Bible is true and historical as well as metaphorically inspired. If it is true in a spiritual sense then what is the necessity to attack other peoples? The contradictions and ambiguities of the Bible that lend themselves to denigration of peoples renders the Bible as a troubling text for its followers and for humanity. Some Jewish and Christian authors try to get around the deficiencies of proving the historicity of the Bible by employing deceptive arguments. One such line of reasoning is a unique argument to support the veracity of the existence of Jews in ancient Egypt. It is referred to as "consequentiality." It is like saying that since we cannot find evidence of the cause (existence of Jews in Ancient Egypt); the present reality (people are following Judaism in the present day) which is ascribed to the cause (for which there is no proof) is proof of the cause. This is the same theory under which Christianity operates in reference to Jesus, and many people have similar customs, beliefs and traditions. It is a form of intensive living in accordance with a fanciful notion of reality that is based on illusion and sustained by ritual and common traditions that unify the culture while overlooking or ignoring non-conforming evidences and histories. This would be like saying that if many people believe that the world is flat it is true.

Those who are in control of society (heads of government and their aristocratic supporters) do not believe in Christianity, or Islam or Judaism or any other religion. They have been born in a cultural religion due to their Ari but their true religion is power and wealth. There can be dictators, despots or tyrants in any culture. The true agenda is to use religion, ethnic differences or other means, to inflame the masses to follow a particular path and to reward their allegiance with material goods. The ignorance, greed and fear of the masses makes them susceptible to the negative suggestions, which are couched in the guise of national security imperatives or messianic religious dogmas that demand the conversion of all human beings in order to ring in some promised land or apocalyptic heavenly condition.

The Limits of Faith

Compounding the issue is the general decline of culture. Consider that the present movement of so-called neo conservatives in the USA of using the government to seek world domination is only the latest incursion. Recall Korea, Vietnam, Haiti, Grenada, Iraq, the conquest of the Americas, the Crusades, etc. the reasons for these wars may be given as spreading freedom or confronting threatening regimes, but since those nations posed no military threat we may conclude that in reality it was about putting down governments that threaten the power to control the world, i.e. megalomania. But to use the term megalomania implies insanity. While it is insane to consider violence towards others, or to pursue unnecessary wealth and pleasure, the movement is more a rationalization of the philosophy of world domination, the world order, under their rule, as they (neoconservatives) have convinced themselves that they are the rightful airs to the Roman Empire whose goal was to control the world. And where the Romans failed they can supposedly succeed because they have the technology.

Note that the move to stir up the passion of the masses with Christianity occurred historically during times of extreme debauchery and lack of ethics in society. Religion was used to rally people towards a common culture and against common enemies and that served the purpose of the ruling classes in each case, for the masses drew little benefits. Note that following each upsurge in religious fervor, material prosperity followed but eventually those societies (Rome, Charlemagne, Catholic Church, Empire of Islam, etc.) declined. What can we say of a culture (United States of America) whose economic status is bankruptcy, which has damaged nature to an unprecedented level? Note that the kind of religious zealotry, dogmatism and fanaticism displayed in the Western religions of the last 2000 years did not exist previously. It grew out of a reaction to extreme violence and degraded morality. So it is an extreme reaction to an extreme social culture. The present movement in USA culture towards intolerance, racism, militarism and religious fundamentalism is just the latest example of this socio-psychological process. As society is beset with more social ills of increasing intensity so to will be the increasing emergence and intensity of orthodox, intolerant and violent religious movements. It survives and thrives where there is ignorance, lack of basic resources (poverty), injustice, miseducation and demagoguery.

The Limits of Faith

In the present, the religious right movement (conservative evangelicals) is being co-opted by the megalomaniacs who are only a small group. But the fears of the conservative Christians are fueled by the fear of degraded culture in society that is fanned by the biblical teachings about hell and damnation. The power elite (president's inner circle, leaders of congress, and heads of multinational corporations) are manipulating the mainline protestants into supporting an agenda to control the world with the incentive of protecting their "way of life." They are after absolute power but they need not wield it like a totalitarian state, an autocracy or a dictatorship like the USSR or Nazi Germany. The indoctrination of the masses by maintaining them in a state of relative economic prosperity with the enticement of someday becoming rich, coupled with the idea that Americans are good and have the best interests of the world at heart and that the USA is the best hope for the world and that the USA is justified or has a right to dominate the world, has become sufficient to elicit a favorable response in the population whenever an alarm is sounded. These mental conditionings, coupled with the trained response to fear of crime, foreign invaders, etc. reinforces the proper response to the propagandistic messages (alarm-fear-anxiety (leading to hysteria)-response-take up arms, shut off critical thinking, do whatever their leaders say). This sounds much like the programming of an automaton, a computer which has a subliminal message that engages when a particular signal has been inputted! It is also similar to the reaction of someone who as been hypnotized, when commanded by the hypnotist. Lest we forget the malnutrition of the standard western diet, that clouds the intellect and destroys the body, it's thinking capacity and its will to follow truth and act righteously!

Primarily it is important to examine such issues so that we may understand the inner workings of the mind and the reasons for its degradation in culture and there we will find the means to be free from those same deficiencies and thereby also discover the path to expansion in consciousness, for that will not happen as long as we harbor illusions about the world or remain choosing sides in the world, who is right and who is wrong. Both the Jews and African Americans in this example are following a false premise that has led them to a fallacious ritual to honor a bogus ideal of freedom since it is their very act which sustains BOTH of their incapacities to achieve true emancipation.

The Limits of Faith

For a serious spiritual aspirants and students of history just saying they are incorrect or ignorant of history is not enough. You can teach history and there are many history teachers around but why is the world in the state it is? Blaming people for their misery is not an option. The misery must be understood thoroughly and then when it is fully comprehended the real solutions will emerge and the means to implement them will arise and when the misery is sufficient the people to follow the higher way will come forth. This is the way of the mystic, the powerful initiate and the discipline of the spiritual masters.

Forgetfulness is a human problem that allows people to follow paths of delusion and those paths lead to actions that are ignorant. As George Santayana said, "those who cannot remember the past are condemned to repeat it." But just remembering is not enough. One must take action based on what is remembered. That action is redressing what was wrong in the past and remaining vigilant to promote truth and righteousness in the future to remain on the path of light and enlightenment. It is the duty of righteous leaders and teachers to remember the past so as to avoid the pitfalls of the past. That is difficult when previous generations die and the new ones forget what pain wars bring. Forgetfulness is like sleeping, a dull state of mind that an aspirant cannot afford.

The Limits of Faith
Christian Colleges and Universities

One important strategy implemented over 30 years ago was to institute the creation of religious right wing Christian Colleges and Universities for educating professionals who would some day take up leadership positions in the society. Universities such as Liberty University and others, are turning out lawyers, social workers, political science majors, health professionals, etc, who will affect public opinion in the areas ranging from welfare to abortion and foreign policy. Those graduates are indoctrinated with the narrow evangelical, or dominionist or otherwise fanatical view of the religious right that would support ideologically extreme views regardless of rational arguments or scientifically proven contradictory proofs. This strategy may be comparable to, but more powerful than, the Neo-con strategy of creating "Think Tanks" that train, put out and support individuals who support the neo-con ideology and agenda, due to the religious fervor of fanatical faith in religious dogma that is involved with the religious following. Those people will have a profound effect on the character of the entire population as they will be diffused throughout the entire population, but the important thing is that they will be in leadership positions that offer them the opportunity to shape public opinion. They would not need to act in collusion overtly, since their common philosophical religious right wing training would effectively make their actions concerted. Therefore, this is perhaps one of the most important challenges that openness and freedom of religion will face in the future.

Theodore J. Lowi, author of *The End of the Republican Era* (Julian J. Rothbaum Distinguished Lecture Series , Vol. 5), and professor of Government at Cornell University, explained that the Republican Party has seized the political discourse and debate and have attained the high ground by putting all issues into moralistic terms. In that way they could frame any argument in terms of morality, meaning right or wrong, good or evil. Thus, the other side has no room to argue a different point of view without then being characterized as being against what is good or right or immoral. Therefore, they have been relatively effective at shutting down dissent from the other party or anyone else who disagrees by using the tactic of labeling the other viewpoints as against morality, and therefore not to be considered or even given any attention. Even though the Republican Party does not live up to its own moralistic rhetoric, it has nevertheless appeared as the party of "values"... and who would want to be against values? The scandal that ensued after political lobbyist Jack Abermoff was found to be bribing members of the Congress for specific quid pro quo actions[58] raised the potential of implicating enough of the republican politicians as criminals that seriously threatened the Republican Party characterization of itself as the party of values.

Thus, the merging of the religious right wing agenda with that of the corporate political agenda in the political leadership has allowed the politicians who are currently in the majority (republicans) to portray themselves as the moral party even though they have engaged in individual and collective activities that are criminal and or immoral. Nevertheless, there have been several contradictions related to the characterization of the Republican Party as the party of values and morality. The same group of neoconservative politicians and religious right wing leaders that often spoke about the sanctity of life and were against abortion to protect life seem to be the same group that most foments war, poisoning children, despoiling the environment, expanding poverty, and promoting deadly AIDS disease transmission [by withdrawing sex education and contraceptives] that has infected millions.

Tim LaHaye, the co-author of the highly successful series of books known as the "left behind series" was the cofounder of the "Federalist Society" in 1982, a right wing think tank that has as its mission to promote conservative judges. The Society has many prominent conservative members, including United States Supreme Court Justices Antonin Scalia and Clarence Thomas, former United States Circuit Court Judge Robert Bork, and former United States Attorney General Edwin Meese. The efforts of the Federalist Society came to fruition in the administration of George W. Bush when two Supreme Court justice vacancies came up. The Federalist Society was responsible for the appointment of conservative judges who are allied to the religious right views, corporate interests, and the elevating of the new Supreme Court justices, John Roberts and Samuel A. Alito, Jr. In an interview with Robert F. Kennedy Jr.[59], Stephanie

The Limits of Faith

Hendricks[60] explained that the placement of conservative judges is for the purpose of *"to have anti-environmental judges in every level of the American judicial system."* Robert F. Kennedy Jr. replied, *"well their ultimate goal is to have corporate control of our society; and it would be laughable except for the fact that there are people who believe in this and have actually achieved very high office."*[61]

Prospects For the Future: Religion Politics, and Economics in the 21st Century

Though there are positive signs in people communicating through the internet, many people awakening to the dangers of intolerance, a growing opposition to the imperialism of the U.S. government, especially in South America, led by Hugo Chavez and Evo Morales, scientific breakthroughs, etc., that does not seem to be translating into effective actions that influence the course of the dominant culture in the world today. That culture seems to be continuing to lead and accelerate the massive despoiling of the environment, promotion of fundamentalism and animosity between cultures, cruelty to animals and humans, and acting politically with impunity to execute its own economic and military designs, regardless of the consequences to the environment, the needs of people, or other countries. Rather, that dominant culture appears to be most interested in protecting the desires of the wealthy and powerful, and following a culturally conservative ideological agenda, controlled by an imperial capitalist political imperative and supported by a religiously conservative and fundamentalist ideology. Consequently, four main disasters loom large on the horizon of human existence that will affect all humanity, but the people of the U.S.A. as well as those countries closely associated with the U.S.A. most strongly. Those challenges are: a religious-cultural conflict, healthcare crisis, financial collapse, and environmental disaster.

The Religious Crisis

Fueled by dominionist ideals, the religious right Christian groups in the United States of America (U.S.A.) have gained political power and have sought to impose fundamentalist religious principles not only on the rest of the population of the U.S.A., but on the rest of the world, which follows the earlier program in U.S.A. history of hegemony through missionary work in other countries, preceded or followed by wars of conquest by the government, or economic devastation of other countries through colonialism or slavery, followed by forced conversions. In the Middle East, Asia and Africa, Islam has achieved important ground in gaining adherents and now, almost 1000 years since the first Crusade wars, the Christians and Muslims are again locked in mortal combat for supremacy over the world, because Islam also espouses an ideal of converting everyone in the world. So on that account alone (contradictory ideologies), conflict is inevitable, yet, the fundamentalists of either side constitute only a tiny minority; but that minority controls the actions of the masses on both sides, which have been purposely miseducated and radicalized by the ruling classes, the secular capitalists, and conservative imperialists, who seek to produce enough wealth and military power to rule (control) the world as if it were their "manifest destiny." In this way, the desires of religiously right wing Christians and capitalist imperial leaders converge and complement each other.

Religious fundamentalism is an ideological perspective that negates any reality that contradicts its viewpoint. Religious fundamentalism is an assertion of certainty in spiritual knowledge that necessarily requires the believer to declare that the fundamental beliefs are true in the sense of historical facts, and because certainties are mutually exclusive [you cannot have two different certainties about the same subject (ex. two different concepts of God) – only one can be correct to the fundamentalist)], then it follows that the particular fundamentalist religion is the "true" and correct one, and all others are false ones. Fundamentalism may also be seen as a fear of uncertainty, and a grasping on to something that provides peace and assurance through certainty. The fundamentalist mind tends towards literalism and focuses on the power of God (or whatever name the Supreme Being is called in their religion) instead of the love of God for its guidance. Therefore, God tends to be seen, by a fundamentalist, as a distant, separate but wrathful divinity instead of a close and forgiving divinity.

Thus, fundamentalism and faith-based religion is a form of religious practice required by those who are unsure of their religious convictions and the nature of reality [Creation], or who may have character flaws they cannot come to terms with or forgive themselves over; this condition renders the personality weak in terms of not being able to stand on its own

The Limits of Faith

without leaning on a power outside of itself for its ability to have a purpose in life or cope and hold on to sanity and peace. The personality is agitated, neurotic, restless and unable to find peace and harmony with itself, the environment or with other human beings, especially those who espouse a different belief system. That insecurity is a source of fear in this personality. The fear acts to cloud the intellect, so the personality focuses on simple teachings [fundamentalism] that can offer assurance. Therefore, the actions of such a personality tends to be fanatical instead of rational, and even if rational arguments are presented to them, they cannot acknowledge or accept them because they destabilize the fragile peace that is being precariously maintained. It is not secure in itself, and therefore tries to find security in the environment by making it reflect a particular ideal of certainty, so it can be assured of the truth, and thereby be internally secure and assured.

Thus, it follows that the need to convert others and eradicate other religions is based on the need for certainty that is confused by the existence of other religions. Thus, it is necessary to block any contradictory information coming from other forms of religion in order to firm up the fundamental beliefs. For that type of personality, it is also therefore important to refrain from participating in or fraternizing with practitioners of other religions, so as to remain free of information that may contradict the fundamental beliefs or concept of reality based on the dogma(s) in which they believe. Finally, if necessary, any information, regardless of its veracity, is to be negated if it contradicts the fundamental beliefs, because the fundamentalist personality cannot risk breaking the fundamental dogmas, as that personality is bound up with them, and would be shattered if the belief system were to be proven false. The fundamentalist personality is so due to weakness, and is supported through constant activity in asserting and promoting the fundamentalist ideas, and avoiding reflection upon them in the context of other religious ideas, for that might lead to critical thinking that could prove error in the tenets, which would shake the confidence in the entire dogma. Following a delusion, be it in politics, religion, economics, etc., in all cases, leads to conflict because the fundamentalist search for certainty cannot be complete until it is the sole reality, and that can only occur when all others are vanquished.

The Limits of Faith

The study of the Crusades is important because it reveals that there was and continues to be deep seeded animosity between Western Christians and the Muslims, which continues to define relations between the two even today. The desire of the west for oil rekindled the ideal of conquering the oil rich countries of Asia Minor. Today, over 600 years after the last Crusade, not much discussion is entertained in the Western media or outside of scholarly circles about the legacy of the Crusades, but in Islamic countries, the mention occurs frequently and without background recapping. This means that when an Arab or Muslim person speaks about the west and references the Crusades, they do not need to explain the history and background about the Crusades to the people to which they are speaking.

Preaching Islam In America[62]
SACRAMENTO, Calif., April 12, 2006

"Almost everyone in the Middle East thinks that America is on a crusade to Christianize the Muslim world, OK. I really hope that is not the case but that's what people believe."

~Imam Mohammad Azeez

In the same news report by CBS, a new poll was presented that demonstrated that fewer than one in five Americans has a favorable view of Islam [19% favorable, 45% unfavorable, 36% no opinion]. Imam Azeez said about the poll, *"it's a stereotype that Muslims themselves must work to change."*

The origins of the Crusades in general, and of the First Crusade in particular, as well as the conflict between the Christians and the Muslims, reaches further back before the beginning of the First Crusade, stemming from events earlier in the Middle Ages of Europe and the first major war between Christians and Muslims.

In the 5th century A.C.E., the Visigoths or Western Goths were barbarian-Germanic tribes who had allied with Rome to keep other barbarians away from the Roman border. As payment for their loyalty, the Visigoths received the territories of Hispania [Iberian Peninsula-now Spain and Portugal] and Southern Gaul.

The Limits of Faith

In 711 A.C.E., the Muslims attempted to conquer Europe, so they crossed the Strait of Gibraltar and attacked the Visigoths, who posed little resistance, and Spain fell under Islamic rule. The Muslims crossed the Pyrenees, and overran the valley of the Rhone. They headed for the Tours, a city in NW central France, on the Loire River, 129mi (208km) SW of Paris. It was the scene of the battle in which Charles Martel defeated the Saracens (Arabs) in A.C.E. 732. The Muslims met the army of the Germans at Tours and were defeated there. Their string of victories in which they overran almost the entire medieval world and North Africa came to an end as they were pushed back into Spain, where they and their descendants remained for over 700 years.

The Crusades were a series of wars undertaken by Western European Christians between the 11th and 14th centuries A.C.E., supposedly to recover the Holy Land from the Muslims. In the 7th century, Jerusalem was taken over by the caliph Umar. In the beginning of that period, Christian pilgrimages to Jerusalem were not cut off at first, however early in the 11th century the Fatimid caliph Hakim began to persecute the Christians and despoiled the Holy Sepulcher [church in Jerusalem, officially regarded as the Church of the Resurrection. It is located in the east central part of the Christian quarter, on the supposed site of Jesus' tomb.]. Persecution of the Christians abated after his [caliph Hakim] death in the year 1021 A.C.E., but relations between Christians and Muslims remained strained and became more deteriorated when Jerusalem passed (1071 A.C.E.) from the rule of the Egyptians, who were predominantly Islamic Arabs at that time, and were considered to be comparatively tolerant to the Seljuk Turks, who also in the same year went on to defeat the Byzantine emperor Romanus IV at Manzikert.

In the late part of the 11th century, the Byzantine Emperor Alexius I, leader of the eastern Christian empire, was threatened by the Seljuk Turks. He appealed to the Western Christians for aid. Pope Urban II started the First Crusade in the year 1095 with the stated purpose of regaining control of Jerusalem and the Christian Holy Land from the Muslims. Records of the campaign reveal that the response turned quickly into a wholesale migration and conquest of territories outside of Europe by both peasants and knights from many different nations of Western Europe. They carried out the call to crusade with little central leadership. They traveled by land and by sea to Jerusalem, and captured the city in July 1099. This was the

The Limits of Faith

only successful crusade. The crusaders established the Kingdom of Jerusalem and some other crusader states.

In central Western Europe at the end of the first millennium A.C.E., there was relative stability of European borders after the Christianization of the Vikings and Magyars. This development gave rise to a class of warriors who then had very little to do except fight among themselves as well as terrorize the peasant population. Outlets for the violence of those groups were promoted in the form of military campaigns against non-Christians. The Reconquista [re-conquest] in Spain was one such outlet. That conflict in the Iberian Peninsula occupied Spanish knights as well as some mercenaries from around other parts of Europe to fight against the Moors.

The Moors were medieval Muslim inhabitants of Northwest Africa, and later of al-Andalus (Arabic name for the Iberian Peninsula including the present day Spain and Portugal), and whose culture is often called "Moorish." The Moors were composed of two groups, Arab conqueror leaders, who were originally part of the leading group that had left Asia Minor to conquer North Africa, and Native Africans [Berbers].

The Muslim conquest of Iberia was managed by Arab caliphates. The soldiery of the first wave of invasions was derived predominantly from Berber peoples [indigenous to Northwest Africa i.e. Black Africans,] of North Africa. Upon conquering the Iberian Peninsula, the Arabs took the best lands and left the inhospitable areas to the Berbers, even though they were all supposedly practicing the same form of Islam. This racism led to protests and conflict that eventually led to disunity and weakening of the Moorish forces. The Visigoth inhabitants, who were now developing the characteristic Christian and Spanish culture, were able to establish themselves in the north and west, and from there eventually extend their control over the rest of Spain by engaging in a conflict that lasted from 718 A.C.E. until finally expelling the last of the Moors from Spain in 1492, the same year that Christopher Columbus was sent to find India but arrived in the Americas in error instead. The apparent success of the Visigoths in Spain, who were gradually expelling the Moors from Spain, along with the abundance of fighters in the rest of Europe, emboldened the Christian Pope to advocate for war.

The Limits of Faith

Thus, history shows that while the lands of Spain and Portugal were conquered by the Romans and then given over to the Visigoths, who by this time had converted to Christianity, the Visigoths lost Spain to the Moors and then won it back again. The Arabs-Berber-Muslims made the first incursions to conquer the land, and at the same time, forced the inhabitants to convert to Islam by imposing a tax on non-Muslims. History also demonstrates that in Spain, as can be seen elsewhere in Arab-Islamic history down to the present situation of the Sudan, the Arab-Muslims tend to force others into conversion and at the same time also practice racial discrimination, segregation and forced miscegenation of conquered populations in order to genetically disperse the conquered population, so as to homogenize it and thereby allow the lighter skinned [Arab descent] leaders to dominate it. In the Sudan, as verified by journalists and nongovernmental organizations, the preferred method of conquest by miscegenation is to murder the male population and rape the women. This is a tactic that the Spanish used in conquering the Native Americans.

AMNESTY INTERNATIONAL[63] 19 July 2004

Sudan

Darfur: Rape as a weapon of war: sexual violence and its consequences

"I was sleeping when the attack on Disa started. I was taken away by the attackers, they were all in uniforms. They took dozens of other girls and made us walk for three hours. During the day we were beaten and they were telling us: "You, the black women, we will exterminate you, you have no god." At night we were raped several times. The Arabs(1) guarded us with arms and we were not given food for three days."

-A female refugee from Disa [Masalit village, West Darfur], interviewed by Amnesty International delegates in Goz Amer camp for Sudanese refugees in Chad, May 2004

1. Introduction
In March 2004, Darfur, Western Sudan, was described by the then United Nations (UN) Humanitarian Coordinator in Sudan, Mukesh Kapila, as the world's greatest humanitarian crisis". (2) Humanitarian organizations operating in Darfur are warning about malnutrition and famine in the region. (3) Today's "worst humanitarian crisis" has been directly caused by war crimes and crimes against humanity for which the Sudanese government is responsible.

The Limits of Faith

The relative calm of Western Europe, overpopulation, the abundance of armies and the desire for wealth [greed] through conquest and expansion led to a rush to conquer other lands besides the "Holy Lands." So on the way to the Holy Lands, the crusaders also sacked the Eastern Roman lands [Byzantium- who were also Christians], as well. Those attacks on Byzantium demonstrate that the motivation was one of greed and not religious. They are not unlike the present day plundering of such countries as the Philippines, Puerto Rico, Venezuela, Panama, Guatemala and others that have a majority Christian population.

The countries of Western Europe did not need to start the crusades. They were wars of choice, not of necessity. Firstly, the west had received calls for help to deal with barbarians from the Eastern church prior to the late 11th century. Why was there no response to those calls? The west did not have the surplus of manpower or internal security at that time, but also their desire for expansion was satiated, up to that time, with internal conquests within Europe. Secondly, if Europeans truly wanted to have the "Holy Lands," why did they not live there to begin with or why did they not move there if the land was so special? Why did they not transfer their population and capital to the Middle East? Why did they remain in Europe? Why did the Western Christian crusaders steal from and kill the eastern Christians with the sanction of the Western Pope? The answer is that the Holy Land, now Israel and Palestine, was not so important in an of itself, but the excuse it offered to move people out of Europe to capture booty, plunder other lands and gain the spoils of war were the better reasons. In other words, the idealism of a religious war for capturing the Holy Lands was not a good enough reason, even though there were some religious zealots who fought for that reason. The profiteering from plundering other countries on the way and capturing new lands was more viable and the Europeans were not ready to do that until the late 11th century A.C.E. So the culture of Europe in the late 11th century was socially and politically driven by religious ideology, and economically fueled by secular greed and the mercantile agenda.

In the 21st century, there seems to be a similar situation unfolding in the conflict between Arab-Muslim nations and nations in Western Europe and the United States of America. In ancient times, the stated desire was to secure the access to the Holy Lands, but in reality it was a land grab and looting of various cities by the kings and peasants of Europe. This time the stated desire is to bring peace to the Middle East, but in reality the purpose is for the U.S.A. to wrest control over the oil fields from Europe, China and Russia, and to stabilize the U.S.A. currency. Supporting President George W. Bush and the conservative Republican Party agenda was the religious right wing fundamentalist ideologies of Pentecostal, dominionist and Evangelical Protestant Christians, the neo-conservative imperialist agenda of world domination, and the corporate agenda of multinational companies seeking to globalize the world economy through privatization of the national wealth assets of other countries and economically subjugating them to the Western economies, to expand profits from worldwide markets.

Pentecostalism is a specific movement within evangelical Christianity that began in the early 20th century. It is typified by enthusiastic religious gatherings and the firm belief that God can empower the Christian for victorious life and service via the Baptism of the Holy Spirit - proof of which is supposedly found in part in the external evidence of tongue speaking. Historic Pentecostalism has its roots in the Holiness Movement and the Revivalism of the "Second Great Awakening" in America during the early 19th century.[64]

> Many secular humanists and fellow Christians criticize some publicly born-again Christians, especially those who became born-again as an overture to entering into politics. They criticize the term, because it allows people to spontaneously become 'Good Christians', and thus receive the uncritical support of a powerful voting bloc, despite the perceived lack of an ethical track record.[65]

As a reaction to the devastation of the Civil War and guilt regarding slavery, rampant corruption, drug abuse, violence and the decline of religious practice in the country, many Christians in the second half of the 19th century felt the country needed a religious revival. Therefore, the fundamentalism that developed in the U.S.A. in the late 19th and early 20th centuries was a reaction to degrading culture that was deteriorating due to low moral values. A similar development occurred in the religion of Islam. In the 18th century, a sect of fundamentalist Islam came into being, which is today referred to as Wahhabism.

Wahhabism in Saudi Arabia began with a surge of reformers seeking to reclaim orthodox Islam from innovation by various sects of Sunni

Muslims. In the 18th century, it spread with the expansion of the First Saudi State under Muhammad bin Saud and his successors.[66]

As a reaction to Western imperialism, many people in the militarily weaker [than the Western government] Arab-Islamic state or states where colonialism or neocolonialism had been imposed in the Middle East have sought power and have founded resistance movements through religious fundamentalism. In this sense, though religious fundamentalism has had a foundation in Arab culture and in the Islamic tradition itself, it has been fomented by Western acts perceived by Arabs as imperialist and as unjust. Due to their military inferiority, many groups resorted to guerrilla attacks and destabilization of the occupying governments by means of surprise suicide bomb attacks in heavily populated areas, which are termed as "terrorism" by Western governments. This term is relative since the Western governments have bombed entire cities filled with civilian populations and have killed far more people than the Arab-Islamic fundamentalist groups. The suicide attacks have been an effective means to neutralize the military superiority of the Western governments [Europe, U.S.A. and Israel], forcing them to negotiate instead of being able to claim outright victory and outright domination of Arab-Islamic populations. The details of how the west helped create and develop Islamic fundamentalism and "terrorism" are detailed in the book *"Devil's Game: How the United States Helped Unleash Fundamentalist Islam"* by Robert Dreyfuss.

Thus, in a sense we are witnessing a modern day form of Crusade via Western attempts to colonize the Middle East, supporting favorable dictators and tyrants or outright military occupations that are further inciting Arab animosity, rekindling old grudges and raising hatred between ordinary Muslims and ordinary Christians that will again endure for decades, if not centuries. The easy military fall of Arab states to western control has given rise to resistance movements that are more intractable. If any Arab state, with deep resentment and will to oppose the Western countries [Europe and the U.S.A.] should achieve or acquire nuclear weapons, they would be surely perceived by the west in general, and the U.S.A. in particular, as a major threat due to longstanding animosities and the dogmatic threats and counter threats by both sides. However, few people reflect upon how countries without nuclear weapons might feel facing the U.S.A., which has used nuclear weapons before and constantly seeks to control other governments by economic or military conquest, causing the weaker nations to seek out the nuclear weapons, perhaps also to protect themselves, by presenting a threat of their own. The case of the conflict between the U.S.A. and Iran is prominent in the present day media. Since the final ouster of the Western backed dictator, the Shah, who was put in place by the U.S.A., the relations between the two countries has been strained, especially due to Iran's refusal to accept Western cultural and political influences, and control of the world economy and the oil of Iran. Consider what would have happened if the U.S.A. had extended true friendship and humanitarian assistance to Iran and sided with the democratically elected government of Iran instead of sponsoring a coup d'é·tat after fomenting social strife and political intrigue? That was not possible due to the U.S.A.'s predilection for control and suppression of other governments in favor of U.S.A. corporations. In this manner, the Western countries [especially the U.S.A in the late 20th century] have promoted, encouraged and supported social and political strife in many parts of the world so as to supposedly prevent them from falling under Soviet influence [during the so called "Cold war"], but in reality to produce weakness in other countries and make them fall under the political influence and economic subjugation of the dominant power, all of which has produced much resentment around the world. The proof of this statement is that after the fall of the Soviet Union, the U.S.A. continued to act as an imperial power, seeking to control the world through direct military force or preferably through manipulation of financial markets and repeatedly not supporting democratic movements, but placing dictators and puppet governments in power.

The Religious Crisis will be caused by ignorance and fanaticism. These cloud the intellect and cause one to become callous, cruel and fundamentalist in one's outlook. To avoid this crisis, there needs to be openness and the realization that religion does not contradict rationality, and anything that is against life and truth is irrational on its face. Anything that promotes hatred and violence is irrational and must be abandoned, whether or not it is contained in a holy book or in a tradition, etc. When the negation of hatred, exclusiveness, and violence are possible, then it will be possible to live by truth, forgiveness and harmony.

As long as nations and governments are influenced by religions that promote exclusivist dogmas and literal interpretations of religious histories that place them as the prominent religion among all other religions or if

The Limits of Faith

they consider other religions to be false, there will always develop strife between the religious followers.

As long as there continue to be those religious followers who insist that others be converted to their religion and that they must be saved and can only be saved through their religion and none other, there will be strife between the religious followers. As long as demagogues are able to control and manipulate populations and as long as there continue to be ignorant peoples who are in search of stability with no prospects for financial justice, social justice or the opportunity to pursue their life in peace and harmony, there will be fertile ground for religious fundamentalist followers.

Therefore, in order to prevent the development of fundamentalism, it is important to promote social and economic justice, including universal healthcare and compassion for all human beings, so that they may not feel the need to resent the rich and powerful who have neglected them, or those who have committed crimes against them by taking their land, mistreating their people, or economically subjugated them.

First Crusade

Jews, identifiable by their Judenhuts,

are being killed by Crusaders, from a 1250 French Bible.

The Limits of Faith

The Western Way of Seeking for Meaning

What is the importance of the questions: Who am I? From whence have I come? What do I seek? And what is the difference between the Eastern versus the Western way of seeking for the answers?

These are fundamental questions that go to the very essence, the core of meaning in life. Many cultures have sought for the answers to those questions because without them there is no meaning in life. If human beings are on earth just to be born, live, procreate and die there is no meaning in that; there is no purpose beyond keeping genes alive for the future, through fleeting moments, passing by until the end of time. What about now? Are we no more than gene transmitters? Are we just conveyors of genetic material for varied ethnic groups or races so that some group or the other may go to heaven and others to hell for eternity?

Eastern, African and Native cultures have sought for the answers by communing with nature and recognizing the divinity in all things, including ourselves through religious processes termed henotheism, pantheism and panentheism. That movement included the ancient Greeks. However, Western culture as it developed with the advent of the three orthodox Western religions (Judaism, Christianity and Islam) moved in a different direction, towards exclusive monotheism, secularism and a scientific method that excluded the imperceptible, yet provable transcendental reality.

In a way, Western science is a form of faith-based religion, having faith only in the observable, the empirical and thus it is exclusive and thus also idolatrous. The idol is the scientific method as defined by Western science. That scientific idolatry leads to bias and a myopic view of the true nature of reality. After the emergence of the Western religions and the takeover of the Roman Empire by Christianity, Western culture developed legends to explore the nature of being beyond the Bible but based on its concepts. The most important of the Western myths designed for the purpose of self-discovery were the Arthurian Legends. Through the characters of the legends and the quest for the Holy Grail the reader was to understand, in terms of Middle Age Europe, how to grow beyond the limitations of the Western society and the rigid church. However, the limitations of the myths reflected the myopic view of the church and the European aristocracy in regards to the nature of virtue and the meaning of spiritual enlightenment, which rendered the Arthurian Legends as weak or primitive means to spiritual evolution in comparison to the ancient African or Eastern texts such as the Pert M Hru of Ancient Egypt or the Upanishads of India.

For many years I have agreed with the importance of the quest for self knowledge, but it was not always so. It is a resounding theme throughout history in all cultures, which I have accepted and try to live. As I have grown older that question took on a more important and serious context. So I set out to explore many schools of thought on the subject but also paying attention to the methods or disciplines for living the quest and achieving the coveted goal of the quest.

The late celebrated and foremost authority on human myth, Joseph Campbell, who wrote extensively on the Arthurian Legends, called the quest a "Hero's Journey" that is dedicated to all human beings so they can live that heroic life as well. That concept sometimes seems daunting because of how the myths portray the heroic characters in impossible situations and surmounting impossible odds. Yet there is an element of heroic quality in all human beings especially when they are not slumbering sheep but see their lives in a wider context of cosmic history. In a way the daunting problems of the world are not unlike the impossible situations of the mythic hero. In that context I adopted the idea of who and what. That is, the question of who am I may be more easily thought of in the form of a duality, in other words, who am I and what am I. To me, Who am I relates to my essential nature, my essential being, beyond qualifications or definitions. Who am I relates to whence have I come? whence have I come relates me back to the source of my essential being, the essence of who I am and in a way the two questions are the same for if I reflect on one I know the other.

What do I seek? This to me relates to what am I. What am I is a statement of what I do, what I have become, what I represent, and that may not represent the who that I am. Many people do not do the things that represent their source, their essential being, otherwise why do people have so many regrets? What am I should flow from who am I. If that were so there would be less conflict within the personality. That conflict is the fundamental struggle of all who have lost their true identity, the who am I, which the relative identities such as John Doe or Mary Doe or the vice president, or butcher, or lawyer, doctor, housewife, etc. cannot resolves. For many the question whence have I come is the opening to wider realization of the meaning of life. For me it has been thus. whence have I come is beyond country, beyond family, beyond relationships and beyond the womb, for all human beings are related in source, having originated in Africa; however, even though those relationships have meaning, some of it may be informative and some which may lead astray.

So these important questions of life need to be reflected upon but also, a guide is helpful. What do I seek is the question all answer in one way or another. Some seek for worldly satisfactions and others spiritual ones, the "know thyself." So initiation, in terms of mystic religion, is a decision that leads to a process of leading oneself to the discovery of the source, the true nature of being to the whence have I come and ultimately to the who am I; Then, after that discovery has been achieved and the journey of discovery is ended, then the reworking of the "what am I" leads to a transformation in purpose in the world. Henceforth, the hero emerges with new understanding, recovered memory and a new reason for carrying on, for the what am I is not sufficient, not sustaining enough, it is fleeting and fragile and so the who am I clamors from within to be known, heard and felt. That is what all want essentially, and that is the birthright of all; and so we are that knight on the quest, the warrior in the chariot as well as the maiden in distress that are to discover the meaning, the reason and glory of the journey, for we already are the destination.

The Limits of Faith

Seeds of Conflict Embedded in the Holy Scriptures

There are several passages in the Western Holy Scriptures that appear to contain ideas or mandates that would inevitably lead those groups to conflict with each other and with other religions. This section will review those statements and attempt to offer insights into their significance and how they may operate to produce strife and conflict among the followers of their respective religions.

Alexandria, the city in Egypt that was founded by *Alexander the Great* upon his conquest of Egypt, became the center of scholarship and learning in the entire ancient world from 300 B.C.E. to 250 A.C.E. It was here that the doctrines of the Religion of Asar (Osiris) and Hermeticism from Ancient Egypt (5,500 B.C.E-300 B.C.E), the Buddhist missionaries from India, the cult of Christos from the Near East and the teachings of Zarathustra (Zoroaster) melded into an amalgam of several Jewish and Christian sects. *Dionysus the Areopagite* played an important role in bridging the gap between the mystical religious teachings, Judaism and Christianity. Up to this time the symbols associated with the Ancient Egyptian Religion of Asar, Hermeticism, and Gnosticism, were known to be metaphors to describe the ultimate reality of the universe and man's relationship to it. It was not until the time of the Jewish leaders who followed Yahweh,[i] Christians from the Byzantine throne and then later, the Muslims who followed Allah (the Supreme Being in Islam), that the symbols and metaphors of religion began to be understood literally, as facts rather than as metaphors to explain the mystery behind every individual. The idea of "God" became circumscribed by a particular doctrine, which was the exclusive property belonging to certain "chosen people." Thus, they saw all other God-forms as idols or devils. All other religions were seen as heresies. Consequently, the followers of those forms were considered as pagans who must be subdued and converted or destroyed. This point is most strongly illustrated in the Bible itself in several passages. This point is of great importance because the concept of a proprietary God is central to Western religions. (Highlighted portions by Ashby)

---

[i] a name for God used by the ancient Hebrews.

The Limits of Faith

The Bible - Genesis 12: 1-3
> "The Lord... said to Abraham... "I will make you into a great nation and I will bless you; I will make your name great, and you will be a blessing. I will bless those who bless you, and whoever curses you I will curse; and all peoples on earth will be blessed through you."

    The above statement from Genesis 12: 1-3 is especially powerful in the light of the emergence of the United States of America and the countries of Europe as world economic and military powers. The slogan "God bless America" is used with prayers, pledges of allegiance and especially at times of war, most recent examples are the Gulf War (against Iraq) and the Afghanistan War (against the Taliban). This statement brings forth the concept that the Jews and Christians are specially blessed by God with prosperity. It essentially says that those who support the Jews and look out for their interests (bless them) are the only peoples on the face of the earth that will receive God's blessing. Thus, with reference to orthodox Christianity, where Jesus is said to be "the only way" to reach God, this verse presents a contradiction to those of the orthodox Christian faith, because it states in no uncertain terms that if any peoples (including Christians) wish to receive God's blessing, they can only do so through blessing (supporting) the (orthodox) Jewish faith. Recall that this statement was written before the time and movement of Jesus, and thus, by accepting the Old Testament as part of their tradition, which includes the above statement, Jesus is apparently not the sole determiner of if Christians will find their way to God. They must apparently first and foremost support the Jews, and thus their religion (orthodox Christianity) is nothing more than an extension of the orthodox Jewish faith: orthodox Christianity = orthodox Judaism + Jesus' teachings. Jesus was born into the Jewish faith, but can he and the ministry he started be considered as being Jewish? If so, there is no need to differentiate between orthodox Christianity and orthodox Judaism. Is Christianity a new teaching? If it is indeed a reformation of Judaic law (Matthew 5:17), can it be said to be in agreement with the old, unreformed Judaic law? Where is the line drawn between Judaism and Christianity? Can it be drawn in the teachings of the New Testament, and if so, then why include sections like the above from the Old Testament? What about other contradictions between the New Testament and the Old Testament, such as the Old Testament teaching (Exodus 21: 22-26), "…life for life, eye for eye, tooth for tooth, hand for hand, foot for foot, burn for burn, wound for wound, bruise for bruise" and Jesus on the other hand teaching (Matthew 5:38-42), "You have heard that it was said, "Eye for eye, tooth for tooth. But I tell you, Do not resist an evil person. If someone strikes you on the right cheek, turn to him the other also," and (Matthew 5:43-48), "You have heard that it was said, "Love your neighbor and hate your enemy. But I tell you, love your enemies and pray for those who persecute you?" The points addressed above are especially significant for Christians who subscribe not only to the contents of the New Testament which are based on the reformist teachings of Jesus, but also on the Hebrew teachings of the Old Testament. Thus, as a result, the above verses in Genesis apply to all Christians who accept the Old Testament. And thus, it follows from the literal understanding of the above verses that the success of any orthodox Christian movement and peoples, and in fact, the very destiny of Christianity as a whole, hinges on the treatment of the Jews by the Christians.

This point is crucial, perhaps to the very survival of humanity in these times of strife where some warring factions have nuclear weapons capability, as this injunction, that those who bless the Jewish nation will be blessed in turn by God, is used to rally people, consciously and unconsciously, especially predominantly Christian countries such as the USA, to the support of the orthodox Jews in their cause of Zionism[i], even when the actions of the Jewish (Israeli) governments are shown to be unrighteous and unjust.[ii] This of course adds fuel to the fire of Muslims who read the verses of the Koran that speak on this issue as it manifested 1300 years ago and obviously continues to this day. Thus, the conflict appears to be religiously, as well as economically based, since the West feels that it needs the oil from the Middle East and to have strategic military bases in those areas (such as in Israel). Also, the West seeks to control and subjugate the peoples of the world, including Muslims. So there is also an ethnic struggle, but underlying this is the deep-rooted religious struggle. (Underlined portions by Ashby)

The Bible Exodus 33 1-2

> "The Lord said to Moses, Go, leave this place, you and the people whom you have brought out of the land of Egypt, and go to the land of which I swore to Abraham, Isaac, and Jacob, saying, "To your descendents I will give it. I will

---

[i] Definition: **Zionism** is a political movement advocating the reestablishment of a Jewish homeland in Palestine, the "promised land" of the Bible, with its capital Jerusalem, the "city of Zion." **Zi·on:** The historic land of Israel as a symbol of the Jewish people. **b.** The Jewish people; Israel. **2.** A place or religious community regarded as sacredly devoted to God. **3.** An idealized, harmonious community; utopia.

[ii] Many actions of the Israeli government have been found by the United Nations to be in violation of international law, such as the creation of settlements in unauthorized territories. See United Nations Resolutions.

The Limits of Faith

send an angle before you, and <u>I will drive out the Canaanites, the Amorites, the Hittites, the Perizzites, the Hivites, and the Jesubites.</u>"

The Bible 2 Kings 5.15
"Now I know that <u>there is no God in all earth except in Israel</u>..."

The Bible - Genesis 1.28
"Be fruitful and multiply, and <u>fill the earth and subdue it</u>; and <u>have dominion over the fish of the sea and over the birds in the air and over every living thing that moves upon the earth</u>."

Numbers 33:50-56

50 ¶ And the LORD spake unto Moses in the plains of Moab by Jordan near Jericho, saying,
51 Speak unto the children of Israel, and say unto them, When ye are passed over Jordan into the land of Canaan;
52 Then ye shall <u>drive out all the inhabitants of the land from before you, and destroy all their pictures, and destroy all their molten images, and quite pluck down all their high places</u>:
53 And ye shall <u>dispossess the inhabitants of the land, and dwell therein: for I have given you the land to possess it.</u>
54 And <u>ye shall divide the land by lot for an inheritance among your families</u>: and to the more ye shall give the more inheritance, and to the fewer ye shall give the less inheritance: every man's inheritance shall be in the place where his lot falleth; according to the tribes of your fathers ye shall inherit.
55 But if <u>ye will not drive out the inhabitants of the land from before you</u>; then it shall come to pass, <u>that those which ye let remain of them shall be pricks in your eyes, and thorns in your sides, and shall vex you in the land wherein ye dwell.</u>

The Limits of Faith

56 Moreover it shall come to pass, that I shall do unto you, as I thought to do unto them.

The preceding statement contains a mandate and a tacit authorization to subdue the earth and control it, displace its current human inhabitants who follow other religions, and destroy the shrines and Temples of other religions. In the extreme, these statements could be interpreted as permission or consent to conquer any and all parts of the earth and its peoples, since their inhabitants are disqualified as being worthy to live or possess property, due to their pagan status, i.e., not believing in the God of the orthodox Jews, and, via extension by accepting the Old Testament teachings as part of their tradition, the orthodox Christians. An atmosphere was created in Europe wherein other peoples could be thought of and classified as "non-human," deserving less consideration and respect.[67]

Verse 55 above is especially chilling to many people because not only does it intimate that it is quite alright (righteous) for the orthodox Jews and other believers of the Old Testament to drive out the inhabitants, but in a subtle way it is also suggesting that the Bible condones genocide, as it is unlikely that peoples currently living in any land will passively give it up and move out, leaving behind their homes, and allowing their religious places of worship and other sacred places to be destroyed, etc., by some invading group. Thus, there will inevitably be war, and thus killing, and so even though the above verse does not speak of committing genocide against other peoples, but rather speaks of "dispossessing" peoples, ultimately, this action must result in genocide, as it is unlikely that the dispossessed group will quietly and peacefully leave their homeland where they have lived for generations, and which is tied to their religious beliefs. Even if they are conquered and must retreat, they will likely spend the rest of their lives, and future generations, plotting retaliation and ways to retake their homeland. The verse states that God is ordering the Jewish people, and by extension, any other religions that accept the Old Testament (i.e. Christianity), to drive people out of their land, and that even if so much as one inhabitant is left on the land, the Jews will live to regret it. This implies that the only remedy to obtain the land "free and clear" is to eradicate all people living there before, so that the people will not exert negative influences on the Jewish people but also so that the descendants will never come to claim the land as their own in the future. As you recall with respect to the history of the Hebrew people, they had seized control of the land of Canaan several times, and were also driven out several times, having not accomplishing the mandate of their Bible, exiling all non-Jewish peoples.

The Limits of Faith

The usurpation of the Americas by the Western Christian countries as well as the colonial expansion into Africa, Hawaii, Polynesia, the Far East, etc., may all be seen as extensions of this apparent Biblical manifest destiny policy which can be understood by another tern, "Imperialism." It is also compared to the current situation between the Jews and the (Muslim) Palestinian people in that the Muslims have been pushed completely out of portions of their land (now called Israel) by the Jews. This is the second time in history that this situation has occurred, the first being when the Jews drove the Canaanites (ancient Palestinians) out of the land in the time before the birth of Jesus. The Palestinian attacks on Israel have been for the most part ineffective, while Israel's reprisals have killed many Palestinians, being highly effective due to the assistance of Western countries and successful investments by Jews abroad which finance the holding of the country (Israel) and its powerful military. The stagnation of the Palestinian nation is tantamount to a living death of sorts in which their misery, as a dispossessed people, is vented on citizens of Israel in the form of "terrorist" attacks and suicide bombings at every opportunity. Some Palestinians have charged that the behavior of the Israeli government is racist and genocidal because of the level of killing that is going on.[68] One would think the situation would be the very opposite, as the Jewish peoples themselves have experienced persecution and genocide. Thus, it would seem that they would be doing everything in their power to ensure what happened to them does not happen to another human being on the face of the earth. Yet, to the contrary, just as the abused child will likely grow up and become an abuser {him/her} self, it appears the victims of genocide have now possibly become the perpetrators. However, it would be seen, from the orthodox Biblical perspective, that the Jewish people not only have a mandate to dispossess every last peoples from their "holy" land, but also a threat that if they do not do so (follow the covenant), God will do to them (the Jewish people) what he instructed them to do to others (i.e. God will dispossess {exact genocide on} the Jewish people): "Moreover it shall come to pass, that I shall do unto you, as I thought to do unto them." Thus, whether unconsciously or consciously, the peoples who follow the Jewish scriptures literally have scripturally impelled themselves to, in the current war with the Palestinians, fight to completely dispossess every Palestinian person from their land, or risk, in their understanding of the scriptures, breaking their covenant with God, thus becoming the dispossessed themselves. Since the Palestinian peoples have no intention of handing over the land to the Israeli peoples, following this scriptural mandate implicitly means that the Israeli people have the right to uses whatever necessary means to accomplish this dispossession, which includes killing. Also, since the Palestinian people have made it clear that they will not leave under any circumstance, then it follows that the only way for the Israelis to rid the land of them completely, and thus be in harmony with Jewish scriptural law, is by committing genocide upon them.

Regardless of whether or not the Israeli people or for that matter, the Christians also, have designs on world domination and the mass conversion of all people, the Bible appears to support that concept. However, they are not alone in this venture of world domination, because similar messages of support for Muslim domination of the world exist within the Muslim history and scriptures. Thus, these two[i] or three religions, depending on how they are categorized, are destined to be at odds, not only with each other, but the whole world, based on the literal interpretations of their scriptures and the historical acts that have been taken by people who follow those religions.

Moreover, the verse above means that any friendly relationships between people of the orthodox Jewish or Christian faiths and members of other faiths, religions or spiritual traditions are inevitably based on false pretenses by the Jewish or Christian person(s) because ultimately their manifest destiny states that they must usurp the lands and dispossess the current inhabitants. It is either that this is the case, or those Jews and Christians are acting impiously (in contradiction to their own edicts to destroy others), and are thus subject to punishment from God. Many Christians and Jews of the orthodox traditions would reject the premise stated above, that they secretly detest people of other religious or spiritual faiths or traditions that they work with or know under other circumstances, and that the relationships are phony, being based on some kind of pretext, yet, by going along and identifying themselves with the orthodox Judeo-Christian religion to any extent implies that this must be so.

With the kind of manifest destiny laid out in the Jewish-Christian Bible, where it is written that God is making a special pact with the people of Abraham and that the land that is currently occupied by the *"Canaanites, the Amorites, the Hittites, the Perizzites, the Hivites, and the Jesubites,* i.e. the Arabs, will be cleared and given to the Jews and Christians, it is no wonder that the Muslim-Arabs in the Middle East felt threatened and continue to feel that there is an impending menace from Israel and the Western countries that are supporting Israel. This feeling is expressed in the statements from the Koran itself (see below) wherein the Jews and Christians are denounced as not being content to live side by

---

[i] As discussed above, with respect to the adherence to the Old Testament, orthodox Christianity can be considered as an extension of orthodox Judaism.

side with those of Islamic (Muslim) faith, but rather feel the need to convert them. They also feel that even if they were to befriend them, the Jews and Christians have their own agenda that does not include the Muslims.

> 2:120 <u>Never will the Jews or the Christians be satisfied with thee unless thou follow their form of religion.</u>

> 3:118 O ye who believe! Take not into your intimacy those outside your ranks<u>: They will not fail to corrupt you. They only desire your ruin: Rank hatred has already appeared from their mouths: What their hearts conceal is far worse</u>. We have made plain to you the Signs, if ye have wisdom.

> 5:54 Section 8. O ye who believe! <u>Take not the Jews and the Christians for your friends and protectors: They are but friends and protectors to each other</u>. And he amongst you that turns to them (for friendship) is of them. Verily Allah guideth not a people unjust.

We need to have a deeper understanding of the history of those who started the religion of Judaism and those who have adhered to it, in order to have a deeper understanding of why the Zionist movement has received such impetus in the mythology, ritual and secular life of Jews. Christians, Jews and Muslims will have a better understanding of Judaism and will also better understand their own position on the Zionist movement. Only correct insight and understanding will allow one to act out of truth and righteousness instead of fear and ignorance. Thus, all peoples will be benefited accordingly.

The Limits of Faith

Reconciliation and Peace Through Religious Reforms and The Complete Practice of Religion

Acceptance cannot come when one sees oneself as superior and others as inferior or when one sees oneself as all right and the other as all wrong. True friendship cannot come from injustice and a true coming together cannot occur if there is segregation of peoples. The idea of race and racism has become intermixed with ideas of religion in orthodox Jewish philosophy. In modern times the idea of racism, which developed out of the European kidnapping and enslaving of African peoples, also adversely affects the Jews. There are Europeans who consider themselves as "white" see the Jews as Semitic or mixed with non-white blood and discriminate against them. As we have seen, from a genetic standpoint, all peoples from the Middle East were of mixed African and Asian descent in biblical times. This was confirmed by Herodotus and other historians of ancient times as well as the writings of the Bible itself. Many people do not realize that there were no "white" or lighter skinned Jews until the latter part of the first millennium of our era (between the fifth and ninth centuries A.C.E.) when the Jews moved into Europe and began to mix with Europeans. It must be clearly understood that Judaism is supposed to be a religion and not an ethnic group or race. This idea is proven easily by the existence of the Falashas, a native Jewish sect of Ethiopia who are dark skinned African peoples, who have been followers of the Jewish faith from a time even before the Jews moved into Europe. More importantly, however, let us not forget that in the remote past, human beings originated in Africa and therefore, all human beings are African in ancestry, just as all humans are of "one blood" (Acts 17:26) and "one flesh" (1 Corinthians 15:39) in God. Therefore, this means that racial distinctions are a bogus and illusory expression of a person's level of spiritual ignorance, a feeling of separation from others which is fueled by frustration, misunderstanding, greed, anger, etc. All human beings deserve compassion, love and caring, regardless of their faith, skin color, etc. Anything less than this is inhuman and un-spiritual, and therefore, in Biblical terms, should be considered sinful. Sin brings on an effect wherein the sinner receives a punishment for the sinful behavior in the form of suffering and frustration, either in this lifetime or according to yoga and other mystical philosophies, a future one. Therefore, those who believe that might makes right or that they have gotten away with something which they know is wrong are overlooking the greater plan of cosmic order which administers absolute justice to all beings. So it is important to be fair, compassionate and forgiving, since those who you treat in this way will more easily be able to respond to you in kind. On the other hand, those whom you have treated badly will in all likelihood treat you with fear, hatred and mistrust in return.

> Job 4:8
> Even as I have seen, they that plow iniquity, and sow wickedness, reap the same.

Around the time of Jesus, Christianity brought in a new message to the Jews. The Kingdom of Heaven was not an exclusive place where only Jews would be able to enter. Rather, anyone would be able to enter if they did what was required, that is, practice the principles that Jesus taught, in their life. This message drew new converts from all lands. It was a principal reason why the Jewish political and religious leaders opposed Jesus, and his teaching which later came to be known as Christianity. Even though orthodox Christianity has been associated with Western civilization and with an elitist church organization based in Rome in the last 1,300 years, it was originally conceptualized as a universal religion. The following passages from Matthew in the New Testament illustrate the universal appeal of Christianity to all peoples. Furthermore, the Gnostic Gospels, Gospels that were omitted by the orthodox Bible compilers in Rome, and other omitted or altered texts[69] show a mystical and ecumenical side to Christianity that is not clearly reflected in the present day versions of the Bible that differ greatly from the original writings which survive from the early biblical text compilers. (Note: there are no original texts of the Bible – we only have copies of them made by scribes, which all differ from each other- so we have many versions and that constitutes another source of strife and confusion about their meanings) So this suggests that the Roman Catholics altered the true meaning of Christianity to suit their purposes.

The Limits of Faith

Matthew 7:21	Matthew 8:11
21. Not every one that says to me, Lord, Lord, shall enter into the kingdom of heaven; but he that doeth the will of my Father who is in heaven.	11 And I say to you, That many shall come from the east and the west, and shall sit down with Abraham, and Isaac, and Jacob, in the kingdom of heaven.

However, the altruistic concepts of Judaism and Christianity are constantly suppressed by many orthodox or dogmatic religious leaders in favor of dogmas and orthodox concepts that are deeply embedded within the Holy Scriptures themselves as *seeds of conflict* (or dissent). These attitudes and the ensuing degradation of the spiritual culture gave rise to policies and practices based on the ultimate idea that Christians cannot rest until ALL human beings are Christians, to establish the "Kingdom of Heaven on Earth," but even in this there is a distinction made between the ethnic Jews, the European Christians (and there is a hierarchy within the European countries and the United States) and the non-Caucasian Christians around the world. In the United States of America, many Christian preachers have criticized and condemned the racial segregation and discrimination that continues even today within the Christian church. This order of hierarchy, which follows along "racial" lines, is denounced in the Koran as well as by non-Caucasian peoples around the world as a hypocritical use of religion to dominate the world.

Thus, these groups need to promote the complete and true practice of religion. They need to move beyond the practice of only the first two levels of religion, myth and ritual, and embrace the third step, mysticism, which will allow them to gain a more universal perspective of their religions, and thus be able to achieve true peace between their religions. Religion has three steps, stages or levels. These are Myth, Ritual and Mystical. Therefore, practices of the non-mystical religions, i.e. religions that do not follow the threefold process of the practice of true religion, are only related to the lower levels of spiritual practice (myth and ritual). This is the level of practice promoted by almost all religions referred to as "orthodox" and/or "dogmatic." This is because, in most cases, the understanding of the religious myth is deficient. This in turn causes people to practice the religion (ritual stage) in a wrong or limited way. In Christianity, the problem is that the main doctrine of Christianity, since the time that the Roman Catholic Church, emphasized the literal interpretation of the life and teachings of Jesus. They hold that he existed as the one and only savior, a real human being who died and was bodily resurrected (literal interpretation). The mystical interpretation is that every human being's soul is Jesus, who has incarnated and been crucified by the world and its desires and distractions, turning it away from the divine vision of its own nature. The resurrection of Christ within the human heart is when the Christ Consciousness or vision of the Kingdom of God is regained. Further, the church doctrine holds that salvation, i.e. seeing the Kingdom of God, must occur through faith in Jesus and by Jesus' returning to the world and digging people out of the grave in order to resurrect them (literal interpretation). The mystical interpretation is that human beings are to grow into Christ Consciousness itself and resurrect themselves by discovering their ability to grow beyond the limiting weight of ignorance and worldly desire.

The belief in the literal interpretation of the scriptures closes the door to understanding Jesus Christ as a metaphor of our own life. With this understanding, or rather, misunderstanding, our own self-effort and responsibility for our own resurrection is negated, being dependent on faith in the existence of a Supreme Being or in Jesus alone. Thus, the last stage of religion, mysticism, is not even part of the spiritual plan of ordinary Christianity as it is understood and presented by most Christians in the world. The reason why people need constant revivals and emotional exuberance to keep them exited and interested is that the limited vision of the church will never satisfy the true yearning of the soul. This is because the worldly philosophy of the church is too limited. The soul, being Divine and infinite, will only find true peace and contentment through a mystical realization of its true nature, which is Divine and infinite. This is the higher message given by Jesus in the Bible book of John 10:34: *Jesus Answered them, Is it not written in your law, I said, Ye are gods?*

So how can we unravel the intricate web of philosophies, faiths, doctrines, customs and traditions in order to discover the true meaning of spirituality in religion which transcends differences which lead to wars and strife? First we must understand what religion is and what its purpose is. Then we need to trace its origins and development. This journey will give us insights into the original intent and meaning, and show us how the forces of politics, economics and history have impacted and changed the doctrines and teachings of religion down to the present. Then we will be in a position to practice religion with an informed intellect and a pure heart which has been cleared of all diffidence.

Arab and Muslim Conquest of Egypt and the Schism between Judaism and Christianity and Between Judaism, Christianity and Islam

The Arab conquest periods of Ancient Egypt includes the Caliphate and the Mamalukes[i] period (642-1517 A.C.E.). Next follows the Muslim Ottoman Turk[ii] domination period (1082-1882 A.C.E.) which was interrupted by the British colonialism period (1882-1952 A.C.E.). In the developing years of Islam ($7^{th} - 10^{th}$ century A.C.E.), there was a fierce conflict between the new religion (Islam) and the previously existing religious practices that existed at the time in Asia Minor, including the remnants of Ancient Egyptian religion and Christianity.

In the Koran itself there are statements that some would even say are conceited or self-important or even arrogant, which like those of the Judeo-Christian tradition, seems to elevate the Muslims above other peoples, especially the Jews and Christians (3:110 Section 12), implying that the Arab culture and people are the most "evolved" form of human being because they best practice righteousness (*"enjoining what is right, forbidding what is wrong"*) when compared to other peoples.

The Muslims "Are the Best of Peoples"

> 3:110 Section 12 (Koran). We are the best of Peoples, evolved for mankind, enjoining what is right, forbidding what is wrong, and believing in Allah. If only the People of the Book had faith, it were best for them: Among them are some who have faith, but most of them are perverted transgressors.

In reading the Koran there is a sense that Islam is protecting itself (and also by extension, Arab culture as well) from the "unbelievers," (4:101 Section 15) who are later described as Jews and Christians, as well as polytheists, and the attempts (of the Jews and Christians) to undermine the Muslims and their way of life for their own nefarious ends (5:54 Section 8). The excerpts also show the philosophical schism between Islam and Judaism and Christianity (2:113 Section 14).

---

[i] Originally they were Turkish and Circassian prisoners of Genghis Khan who were sold as slaves to the sultan of Egypt, who trained them as soldiers. They fought for Egypt but then seized power. (Random House Encyclopedia Copyright (C) 1983,1990 by Random House Inc)

[ii] Ottoman Empire – empire by Arabs from Turkey that controlled Asia Minor for 600-years (13th century to early 20th century.)

The Limits of Faith

Unbelievers are the enemy

> 4:101 Section 15 (Koran). When ye travel through the earth, there is no blame on you if ye shorten your prayers, for fear the Unbelievers may attack you: For the Unbelievers are unto you open enemies.

> Animosity between the Muslims and the Jews and Christians
> 2:111 (Koran) And they say: <u>"None shall enter Paradise unless he be Jew or a Christian."</u> Those are their (vain) desires. Say: "Produce your proof if ye are truthful."
> 2:112 (Koran) Nay, -- whoever submits his whole self to Allah and is a doer of good, -- he will get his reward with his Lord; on such shall they grieve.
> 2:113 Section 14 (Koran). <u>The Jews say: "The Christians have naught (to stand) upon"; and the Christians say: "The Jews have naught (to stand) upon."</u> Yet they (profess to) study the (same) Book. Like unto their word is what those say who know not; but Allah will judge between them in their quarrel on the Day of Judgment.

In order to counteract the missionary, and expansionist designs of the Jews and Christians, the early followers of Islam, beginning with Muhammad, incorporated statements about the Christians, characterizing them as "enemies" and describing how they seek to convert the Muslims and all people to their faith with the idea that *"None shall enter Paradise unless he be Jew or a Christian"* (2:111) and other similar tenets. The Koran contains responses that the "believers," the Muslims, should give to the "unbelievers" (Jews and Christians). The statements belie fundamental differences between the three groups and also the political necessity to resist the Jews and Christians in order to sustain the Islamic faith, to the degree that the Jews and Christians are mentioned specifically and their actions are described in detail. The Koran states emphatically that the Jews and Christians can never be satisfied with anyone who does not believe as they do (2:120), and that the Jews and Christians say that in order to "be guided" to salvation (2:135), the Muslims must "become Jews or Christians" (2:135). One of the main contentions is the belief that Jesus is the son of God. To this the Muslims are to reply to the Jews and Christians that "we believe in Allah" and the revelation given to the prophets (of the old Bible) and that "we make no difference between one and another of them (prophets): And we bow to Allah (in Islam)" (2:136)

The Limits of Faith

Struggle Against the Jewish and the Christian Missionaries[i]

    2:120 (Koran) <u>Never will the Jews or the Christians be satisfied with thee unless thou follow their form of religion.</u> Say: "The Guidance of Allah, -- that is the (only) Guidance." Wert thou to follow their desires after the knowledge which hath reached thee, then wouldst thou find neither Protector nor Helper against Allah.

    2:121 (Koran) Those to whom We have sent the Book study it as it should be studied: They are the ones that believe therein: Those who reject faith therein, -- the loss is their own.

    2:135 (Koran) <u>They say: "Become Jews or Christians if ye would be guided (to salvation)." Say thou: "Nay! (I would rather) the Religion of Abraham the True, and he joined not gods with Allah."</u>

    2:136 (Koran) Say ye: "We believe in Allah, and the revelation given to us, and to Abraham, Ismail, Isaac, Jacob, and the Tribes, and that given to Moses and Jesus, and that given to (all) Prophets from their Lord: <u>We make no difference between one and another of them: And we bow to Allah (in Islam)."</u>

    2:137 (Koran) So if they believe as ye believe, they are indeed on the right path; but if they turn back, it is they who are in schism; but Allah will suffice thee as against them, and He is the All-Hearing, the All-Knowing.

Verse 5:54 Section 8 is an injunction to not befriend either the Jews or the Christians or allow them to be "protectors" of the Muslims (i.e. government leaders) as they have their own interests ahead of anyone else's. Verse 3:118 goes even further, stating that the words of the "People of the Book" (i.e. Jews and Christians) are "Rank hatred" and what "their hearts conceal" is even "worse." Verse 3:119 is very telling in its implications. It states that even those Arabs who converted to the "whole of the Book" (Bible) have been mistreated by the Jews and Christians. This expresses extended dealings between the Muslims and the Jews and Christians and also implies the underlying ethnic differentiation that was made by the Jews and Christians which has been evident throughout history in the dealings between the Jews and Christians and other groups from around the world, including Native Americans, Africans, Asians, etc. Thus, a component of segregation that later contributed to the development of racism appears to be

---

[i] One who attempts to persuade or convert others to a particular program, doctrine, or set of principles; a propagandist.

The Limits of Faith

present in the concept of the early Jews and Christians, and this insincerity and duplicitous ulterior agenda further gave impetus to the rise of Islam in the Middle and Far East as well as North Africa.

> 5:54 Section 8 (Koran). O ye who believe! <u>Take not the Jews and the Christians for your friends and protectors</u>: They are but friends and protectors to each other. And he amongst you that turns to them (for friendship) is of them. Verily Allah guideth not a people unjust.
>
> 3:118 (Koran) O ye who believe! Take not into your intimacy those outside your ranks: <u>They will not fail to corrupt you. They only desire your ruin: Rank hatred has already appeared from their mouths: What their hearts conceal is far worse</u>. We have made plain to you the Signs, if ye have wisdom.
>
> 3:119 (Koran) <u>Ah! Ye are those who love them, but they love you not, -- though ye believe in the whole of the Book</u>. When they meet you they say, "We believe": But when they are alone, they bite off the very tips of their fingers at you in their rage. Say: "Perish in your rage; Allah knoweth well all the secrets of the heart."

Verses 3:118-9 give the impression that the early Muslims felt the pressure of the Jewish Christian movement trying to encroach on the Muslim territory and religious life. The introduction of the Jewish state into Palestine without regard to the population of Palestinians there, forcibly displacing people, and then suppressing their protests while at the same time preventing their development of their economy and infrastructure, has been likened by many Arab-Muslims in present-day Islamic countries (especially Palestine) to a form of racism[70] that is expressed in the form of Zionism[i], which is practiced by Western countries towards populations composed of non-Caucasians.

The following verse from the Koran is significant because it appears to state in no uncertain language that the teachings brought to the world by the "holy Apostle" (Muhammad) "supercedes" that of the Jews. Verse 9:30 Section 5 specifically takes issue with the Christian idea that "Christ is the son of Allah" and that in this they *"imitate what the Unbelievers of old used to say."* This statement refers to the Ancient Egyptian religion, as Heru, the savior and prototype for the Christian Christ figure, was also stated to be the son of God (Asar, Osiris). The Muslims see this concept as a great "delusion" coming from "their mouth" i.e. not from revelation.

---

[i] An organized movement of world Jewry that arose in Europe in the late 19th century with the aim of reconstituting a Jewish state in Palestine. Modern Zionism is concerned with the development and support of the state of Israel.

The Limits of Faith

Thus, the Islamic faith seeks to put down and invalidate the Jewish and Christian faith just as they too seek to put down and invalidate Islam. These three religions therefore, are scripturally gridlocked in a vicious cycle of disharmony and conflict. As the seeds of dissension and disharmony are embedded in the scriptures themselves, despite the attempts to promote harmony and peace between the religions, there will ultimately be an incompatibility that will lead to conflict.

This conflict is even more pronounced when the views of these three religions, which consider themselves to be "monotheistic" are considered in so far as their relations with what they consider to be "polytheistic" religions such as the Kamitan and the Hindu religions. There is more denigration, more invalidation and hence more rejection and violence directed at those religions. So while many people claim that Islam is a religion of "peace" because the word "Islam" which means "submission to God" is related to the word for peace, in reality there can be no peace when such statements are included in the religious faith. They inevitably lead to a separation and a competition between faiths, as long as there are people who believe in the scriptures literally as a historical reality or as a dogmatic injunction regardless of its apparent irrationality or the contradictions them may have with empirical evidences or other objective evidences. Since there is no way for these religions to continue without their "holy scriptures" and the prospect of amending them is virtually nil, then it follows that there can likely be no permanent resolution to this problem. A permanent resolution can only occur if these aspects of the scriptures are expunged, and if that were to happen, it would present a contradiction to the orthodox followers since they regard the "whole scripture" as a "divine revelation," which, to them, means that the entire scripture is "true," and "perfect," and thus must be followed in its entirety.

> 9:30 Section 5 (Koran). <u>The Jews call Uzair (Ezra) a son of Allah, and the Christians call Christ the Son of Allah. That is a saying from their mouth; (In this) they imitate what the Unbelievers of old used to say. Allah's curse be on them: How they are deluded away from the Truth!</u>

Thus, faith alone in a scripture cannot be the sole form of validation given to it. Faith or belief in a tradition or philosophy alone can lead to dogmatism and fanaticism that can be manipulated into conflict and untold human sufferings.

Is Reason Born out of Faith or Does Faith Come Out of Reason?

How can we understand the mysteries of faith in terms of pre-Judaic/Christian/Islamic concepts of faith-based religion? The ancient Greek concepts involve Logos, Eros and Psyche. Some aspects of these were adopted by the Jewish and Christian theologians but not completely or with full understanding of their deeper implications. This fundamental question, *Is Reason Born out of Faith or Does Faith Come Out of Reason?* Is one which goes to the heart of what it means to be human, both intrigues and confounds at the same time in a way. If we are to say that faith is the antecedent of reason then is it rational to have faith at all? Do we not need reason to realize we need to have faith because we realize that our reason is not sufficient to lead us to the truth? In the Arthurian legends, there is a wonderful display of the search for self-discovery and meaning that is expressed through ancient lore, magic and the glory of chivalry, through the Holy Grail, the struggle of personal desire versus submitting to authority or the fate that has been outlined by society versus the roles people imagine for themselves. Yet, but for the distance from ancient Greek culture, would not Western Culture have skipped the gloomy saga of the dark or middle ages and risen beyond the question? Would it not have already progressed to the adoption of logos and moved forward from there, not necessitating the rediscovery of Greek Philosophy?

It seems as though humanity or at least it's segments which become disconnected from their original source cultures have a way of degenerating to the point of having a crisis of faith that necessitates the recreation of a myth, a legend that enlightens the quest for the meaning of life through reason. It might be said that the process of death causes forgetfulness, yet at the same time death is what allows progress.

The Limits of Faith

But if we accept that Logos is the cognitive reflection of the underlying order of the universe that exists in the essential nature of humanity then is it not true that logos is the source of itself? In other words, reason is the capacity that allows awareness of reason or at least a clue of order or the shadow of doubt about the underlying organization of nature.

Yet the struggle of humanity belies its efforts to move towards enlightenment. The post Enlightenment period conceptualization of reason, or logic as an empirical process is a departure from the Logos conception of the Ancient Greeks. And again, in the twentieth century and the beginning of the twenty-first human culture finds itself immersed in religiosity in search of meaning but encountering increasing conflict within itself and with nature.

Western culture, as the leading policymaker of modern times places as much faith in religiosity as in self-reliant power and that power to discern the orderliness of nature has been used to manipulate natural resources towards economic advancements. Thus the faith or desire of wealth and power and pleasure has surpassed the search for the Grail or the Tao or the inner meaning of the Logos. If the ancient Greek philosophers would say that the world is rational, would Corporate America's philosophy of the rationality of dumping waste into rivers is rational be equivalent? What makes reason reasonable? What makes it true? For the unscrupulous businessman there is logic in dumping. Is not the swollen bank account of the businessman proof of his philosophy of irresponsibility and should he not love that philosophy as a philosopher of business? It may be a superficial or self-serving reason but it is reason.

Love of philosophy therefore may not be enough to make one a true philosopher. As Parmenides put it, there is something that comes before even philosophy and that is what is. So philosophy can only explain what is but the philosopher's love must be for what is ultimately and not what is conveniently. Therefore, reason is more than what can be proven through "observation, experimentation, or abstract reasoning as the foundation for the validity of its conclusions"; it is indeed what comes before and makes philosophical speculations possible, namely what is perceived, the perceiver and the process of observation. The question also comes: what is proper observation, for as modern physicists tell us, the act of observation changes what is perceived. In like manner, the Grail, the Tao the Shuniya

The Limits of Faith

of Buddha or the Anrutef of the Ancient Egyptians is unfathomable, yet its manifestations are replete with orderliness; yet we can say no more beyond that, for as a wise one once said, we are using the second best thing to describe the first. So in this way we might proceed thus, only when we lose the question will we achieve the answer but before we lose the question we need faith to ask it and before we stop asking the question we must be at peace in resolute order, harmony and peace and when we have lost the sense of order and the need for the question the answer is revealed as itself.

If Psyche cannot live without Eros because Love must dwell with the Soul, because the Soul animates all things, and if the Soul needs Eros because there is no meaning in life without desire there is need for Logos, for without order or reason for their togetherness there is no capacity for existence. Yet it is the myth of Psyche and Eros that reflects to us the underlying reality through Logos since they are not realities but reflections of what exists and Logos allows us to understand them and ourselves also. Thus, in terms of Logos, which rises beyond rationality to oneness with Creation, and Eros, which is impetus for love of essence [Psyche], the soul and logos are therefore one and the same since Eros-Psyche {love of soul} as philosophy {love of wisdom} leads to understanding essence, thus understanding essence {soul} and essence itself are one and the same.

They are one and the same in the same way as lovers who seek each other for completeness, fulfillment, etc. Logos is the underlying order of creation and as well the source of understanding which is the soul of all i.e. psyche. They seem go in different directions, to operate with different energies in Creation and the human heart, but that is a deviation from their original essence which must inevitably come back together again and indeed they desire to come together through Eros because they are originally one. So just as two lovers seek togetherness to complete each other, they too seek togetherness and they operate through us and all things for all in creation is dual but beneath the duality there is underlying oneness.

The Limits of Faith

I or Thou?

Martin Buber has been described as a "utopian Zionist." He strongly believed in the capacity for Zionism to change relationships between people. It is notable that he wrote forcefully in favor of the rights of Arabs in Palestine and he worked towards the establishment of a shared Jewish-Arab state. That ideal seemed to be a strong goal for him and even though it failed, in his time, it is a monument to his work and to him as a human being of ethical consciousness. Martin Buber's *I and Thou* is an extensive analysis of how human beings perceive and interact with reality is fascinatingly similar to Buddhist and Vedantic teachings related to the ego and to perceptions of reality through *maya* [cosmic illusion]. Thus it is not surprising that he studied Cabbala philosophy, which may be regarded as Jewish Mysticism, a form of philosophy that goes beyond the ordinary orthodox and constricted form of Judaism.

His exposition outlines very philosophically but accurately, the difference between perceiving the world as objects as opposed to essence of related self-being. Simply put it is a philosophical conception is the relationship of I with other either as "It" or as "Thou". The "It" is objectified relation in reference to the ego self. The "Thou" is unconditioned but at the same time communal relation with the other in reference to the enlightened ego self. Essentially the philosophy outlines how egoistically relating to objects and people, as things to get something from or manipulate, lead to limited relations. On the other hand, relating to the world and people as extensions of self leads to greater understanding and fulfillment in relationships. If we approach relationships with the perspective of their being thou we can have the possibility of partaking in a higher communion with them, experiencing beyond the phenomenological aspect of the ordinary ego driven experiences. But that higher experience cannot be manufactured, but one must be open to the essence in order for it to reveal itself.

The Limits of Faith

"One of the main struggles of human existence is between self-identity and group membership...
 Humans are social animals and generally depend on each other to provide context and meaning...

-Martin Buber

Question:

About the statement: "On the other hand, relating to the world and people as extensions of self leads to greater understanding and fulfillment in relationships."

Depth psychologist, James Hillman, would argue that that would merely be strengthening the ego, because everything would be merely extensions of the self. He promotes something like a return to our mythological past where the gods were gods and not merely archetypes contained within one personality that is identified with the ego.

Answer by Dr. Ashby:

OK, I would agree with the above in terms of egoistic relationships, that those could be extended into the world and one could even become deluded about the world based on one's own projections on the world of one's own egoistic vision. However, if we look more in terms of Buber's ideal of relating to the world and with people as extensions of a greater self, like the sum of the parts equal more than the sum. In other words, relating to the universe as a greater aspect of self that holds more than the perceptions of the ego senses and mind through relating with the universe as something "more than what I want" and letting it, even accepting it as it express itself as it means to and allowing the meaning to manifest. If we consider the writings of Black Elk in *Black Elk Speaks"* that's what Black Elk may have experienced, that in describing his visions and the glory of those experiences he seemed to lose that glory but for the pursuit of the redemption of his culture. So he may have actually been experiencing his Thou but personally missing it because of looking for a phenomenological outcome?

The Limits of Faith

Question:

I"I see, so the identification with self is more like the Brahman/Atman ideal? All is seen as part of Brahman."

Answer by Dr. Ashby:

Ideally I would say yes but I would not expect that from an ordinary person, untrained in advanced philosophy. I was still thinking in terms of Buber's path of just realizing that there is more than the little "me" and I think that eventually that would lead to true selflessness and also extending true friendship and communion with others, nature and with the Divine in the Vedantic self. So I think there is a lot of value in Buber's work to lead the western mind to a place where it will be more peaceful and egalitarian as well as spiritually enlightened. I also feel that the Native American path of visioning and trance can lead to the same higher awareness but I think that the cultural devastation caused by European conquest, domination and purposeful murdering of Native American leaders has severely damaged the philosophical insights that the elders brought to the culture. So it is important to maintain a separation between the visioning process, the process of self-discovery and the political, socio-economic struggles of a people. Yet there is a relationship between them. The great personalities of all ages and all cultures have influenced humanity out of their inner experiences and insights into the nature of being which manifested as true humanitarian caring for all humanity. In order to achieve that level of consciousness they had to free themselves from the very things that engendered the struggle in the beginning, human degradation, conflict and strife; but that inner journey allowed them to serve humanity in a most dynamic and powerful way that would not have been possible if they had been caught up in the struggle on a psychological level.

The Search For Reality

In Western culture the search for what is reality has taken many forms. Philosophers such as Rene Descartes contributed greatly and were very influential in the developing Western thought processes in the effort to discover meaning. In order to understand the Western mind, how can we compare and contrast Descartes' thought experiment with his demon in *Meditations on First Philosophy*[71] and the character Lancelot's[i] difficulties in the *Quest for the Holy Grail?* The exploration of this question will also provide insights into the nature of what people have faith in and the illusoriness of the physical world which they regard as physical, historical and finite.

The philosophical exploration of what is "Reality" is perhaps one of the most fundamental questions of human existence and yet much of this investigation is relegated either to theologians or quantum physicists. Most theologians do not really explain the nature of reality and just present dogmatic pronouncements about the creation of the universe by God without explaining where the material came from which God used and also where God came from. The physicist have developed elaborate theoretical constructs based on experimentations such as the particle acceleration and collision experiments that show how matter is actually empty space and actually is not material, but appears so due to the vibratory state of the energy that it is composed of. In this contexts, the thought process of philosophers such as Descartes, who developed the famous adage *cogito ergo sum,* ("I think, therefore I am") seems well supported in that as Descartes found, through his reflections, the senses are illusory or the sense perceptions are untrustworthy. This problem of course, affects all human beings who believe in the reality of their sense perceptions as this guides their thought processes and are therefore, unlike Descartes, led by their senses instead of looking at sense perceptions objectively. Plato's analogy of the cave illustrates this predicament of the human senses and how they distort the perception of reality. Plato sought to illustrate how a particular means of awareness leads to misperception of

---

[i] Arthurian Legends

The Limits of Faith

reality. In this way to modern yogis from India (especially the creators of the Bhagavad Gita text) and the mystery practitioners of Ancient Egypt (especially the creators of the Pert M Hru [Book of the Dead] text)and many other cultures have sought to teach those human beings who are ready to accept it that the physical reality is nothing more than a perception of the senses. This is important because as the mind is colored by its desires or cultural, religious perspectives, the illusion of the senses can distort those cultural or religious perspectives leading to misapprehension or misapplication.

In the Grail quest, Lancelot is caught up in the perception of reality based on his knightly duty as well as the perception of the ideal of courtly love and the ideal of spiritual pursuits. Those themes seem to reverberate down through history into the present developments of western culture, as evinced in many warped relations between men and women and the conflicted search for power, to be the "knight in shining armor" and at the same time to discover "true love" even if that might require adultery. The modern day divorce rate which exceeds 60% may also be considered as a legacy of the western ideal of courtly love and the struggle with theological ideas about love and sex that preceded the church and the Arthurian legends and an effect of the continuing misconception of reality that most people live with.

If we were to accept that reality is not what the senses perceive then we would have a very different outlook on life, not allowing ourselves to fall for the seemingly enticing objects of our seeming desires. That would be reason and certainly Lancelot would have been benefited from that. However, we are still left with the question of what or who is the perceiver who is doing the perceiving? Descartes gives us:

> 8. But what, then, am I? A thinking thing, it has been said. But what is a thinking thing? It is a thing that doubts, understands, conceives], affirms, denies, wills, refuses; that imagines also, and perceives.
> *Meditations on First Philosophy*
> by **Rene Descartes**

Descartes discounts the senses as being untrustworthy because they are illusory, appearing to be real in a dream as in the waking state of the mind.

The Limits of Faith

Nevertheless he proceeds to assert that the thinker of the thoughts or perceiver of perceptions is real. If we are to accept that the sense perceptions are illusory and that is evident from the inconsistency of the reality they present, then how can we assume that the perceiver of that illusion is real? {*cogito ergo sum,* ("I think, therefore I am")}. How can Descartes also say that there is a beneficent god that exists if he is using the illusory senses to think about God? If he cannot think about God without using his senses then how can he assert the existence of God or anything else for that matter? It sounds like an assumption that there must be something real somewhere because even though one may be perceiving illusions the perceiver must be real, etc. Yet that is not a reality, just an assumption. Eastern schools of philosophy have grappled with this question for hundreds of years before Descartes and Plato. In describing the images of reflections perceived by hypothetical persons in a cave, Plato was actually acknowledging the wisdom of the illusoriness of sense perceptions.

> … and then conceive some one saying to him, that what he saw before was an illusion, but that now, when he is approaching nearer to being and his eye is turned towards more real existence, he has a clearer vision, -what will be his reply?
>
> *Republic* by Plato

Plato was also pointing out that the illusion is actually a reflection of the higher reality that is missed by most persons who do not apply themselves to philosophical researches. The Vedantic sages of India concluded that the universe is a manifestation of Maya or cosmic illusion, in which God manifests as the phenomenal reality which is illusory. Thousands of years earlier the Ancient Egyptian sages concluded similarly that reality is a modification of undifferentiated matter, termed *Nun* or primeval ocean. The mystics of the East (India) and South (Africa) and West (Native Americans) realized that all reality is a manifestation of a transcendental entity but that assertion does not come from dogma or highly informed reflections on theoretical mental constructs. It is based on the experience of what mystics have described as their experience once they were able to transcend the mind and senses through the process of deep meditation. They found that after a time of concentrating the mind on one thought the mind ceases to "think" and all that is left is awareness without differentiation, without qualification, without duality or separation between knower, knowledge and objects. In that condition the mystics of all cultures have reported a unitary underlying basis for all reality. That is the substratum from which arises the phenomenal reality in the form of a distorted reality, like a mirage. But as Plato stated, a person whose attention might be turned away from the illusion to see the reality that the illusion is a reflection of, would have much difficulty in accepting the true reality. In the same way, most people are far removed from the true or "absolute" reality. Their perceptions of self-identity are convoluted with their perceptions of the world and so they see themselves as caught up in the struggle of life with no exit or higher reality to explore. They are therefore bound by their desires, those being part of the illusory world that they believe in, so they feel compelled to act on emotions which are themselves based on erroneous thinking of reality, and also influenced by hormones and other environmental factors which are also parts of the illusion. So they may believe their feelings are their own, their situation in life is their own and that all occurs by fate or blind luck, etc. When bad things happen or when the personality is led to "sinful" behaviors it is often attributed to a third party affecting the personality or to fate.

> 12. I will suppose, then, not that Deity, who is sovereignly good and the fountain of truth, but that some malignant ***demon***, who is at once exceedingly potent and deceitful, has employed all his artifice to deceive me; I will suppose that the sky, the air, the earth, colors, figures, sounds, and all external things, are nothing better than the illusions of dreams, by means of which this being has laid snares for my credulity
> Meditations on First Philosophy by **Rene Descartes**

In a way the struggle of Lancelot may be seen as a person who is helplessly acting on the desires of their heart that are real to them, the denial of which would be denying something real. Descartes would say that the struggle is due to an outside force, a demon who is acting to hide the reality from him. This is very much like the idea promoted by present day evangelical and fanatical Christians who refuse to believe in the science of Geology which has shown by carbon dating and other means, that the world is much older than 6,000 years old. Yet the fundamentalists say that that is either scientists who are fooled or due to God testing their faith by presenting contrary information through science. So therefore, science, which is limited but nevertheless, the best instrument for knowing phenomenal reality, is discounted or violently objected to; hence the struggle between creationists and evolutionists. Descartes' statement is much like that of the popular comedian Flip Wilson who used to be fond of saying "the Devil made me do it." That conception, being illusory, is incorrect and has the effect of rendering the mind pliable and weak to the temptations of life by assigning responsibility elsewhere and not reflecting on the consequences of actions.

The troubles of life can be traced to erroneous forms of thought which are based on illusory perceptions and trust and belief in these as abiding realities. By thinking based on illusion, human beings entertain, focus on and act on ideas that form a complexed personality. Believing the world is real leads to believing that one's personality and its desires are real and then follows that one will feel compelled to act on the subjective realities of the mind in order to "find happiness" or discover one's "destiny". What ensue are entanglements, and complicated schemes to pursue the objects or situations of one's desire. When those objects or situations are not achieved the personality feels anger or hatred at what it perceives as the obstacle to achieving the fulfillment of the desires. If the objects or situations are achieved then the personality develops greed and wants more but also there is tension because of the fear of losing what has been attained. This has been a source of untold miseries for individuals as well as nations through the actions of demagogic or power hungry political or religious leaders throughout history.

The mystics of ages past as well as those of the present do concur on the point that in order to know reality it is necessary to transcend the mind and senses. In order for that to happen there needs to be virtuous character, balanced personality and as the ancient Greek philosophers would say "love of knowledge," or "love of wisdom," as in "philosophy" which uses the Greek "Philos" meaning love based on spiritual kinship.

However "Love" as in philosophy needs to be directed at truth, at what is real and that makes a true philosopher. In order to be a true philosopher according to this ideal means loving what transcends that which is illusion so by definition a true philosopher loves what transcends the mundane, phenomenal and illusory reality perceived by the mind and senses and

The Limits of Faith

what people perceive as good or evil based on their desires or cultural allegiances. Having cultivated that desire that personality rises above the illusion to discover the real, to turn away from the shadows that Plato described, turn away from the complexed fate of worldly minded seekers of pleasure in the world of time and space and thereby they discover freedom from fancies of the mind. In that sense, the Grail legends attempt to point out the folly of human indulgence in egoistic desires based on worldly knowledge and the path to what is truly holy and real. That is the message of all mystics of all cultures in all times. However, unless the pursuit of truth becomes the purview of the common man and woman instead of being reduce in importance and consigned to ethnologists and theoretical physicists and denigrating others who voice such ideas and condemn them to an undesirable fate such as Socrates was, the path to truth as well as the prospect of peace and harmony for humanity will remain a distant and unattainable longing.

Question:

All of us have come to this class with our own preconceived ideas of what is real and what isn't. As a class we could then use reasoning and metaphoric imagery to collective agree or disagree on what ever we want. We could then have our class values and what we think is real.

Answer by Dr. Ashby

I agree with your basic premise about the values and ideals that people hold dear as the source of their perception of reality; At least from a cultural and perceptual perspective or relating to the world. The idea of everyone in the class collectively potentially agreeing on a subjective reality is also inspired. But of course that reality would be illusory or as real as people in a different group. These reflections relate me to what is beyond the subjective to what is objective.

Question:

"But to give you advice would profit you nothing in your present state, for it would be like the man who builds a tall, strong tower on shifting

The Limits of Faith

ground; and it happens that when the work is well advanced, the whole edifice come crashing down." (Quest, p.90).

Lancelot was not ready for reason until he was free of his demons. "The devil showed me the sweets and the honey, but he hid from my eyes the everlasting woe that lies in store for him who treads that road to its end" (p. 88). His soul was guided by his love for Guinevere and it was "For her love alone I accomplished the exploits with which the whole world rings" (p.89). Therefore, no, reason would not have helped Lancelot until he could free himself of his demons.

Answer by Dr. Ashby

I would like to add that I see Lancelot's demons as his misconception of reality but from a fundamental perspective. If he was guided by his love of Guinevere that is the pursuit of an illusion, which renders the intellect atrophied. Rather he should have been founded (guided) in the pursuit of truth, then in that "state" of mind the wisdom would have been useful to him. While it is true that when motivated by certain passions men and women can do incredible feats. But when we look at history we mostly remember those who achieved incredible feats in the field of religion and philosophy and not those of worldly pursuits such as love, sex, money, power, etc. This is because history has demonstrated that the genius of human beings can be applied to destructiveness more easily than Creation and there is an innate recognition that creation, harmony and peace are more valuable, closer to the nature of the universe and therefore closer to truth.

Question:

This reminds me of the "quest.' But having finished the book I am not so sure that hatred is produced by nonattainment of the grail or that achievement produces greed and want. Are you to tell me that Moses, Jesus, Buddha, Mohammed, or the like wanted more or could be labeled greedy?

The Limits of Faith

Answer by Dr. Ashby

I would say that along with or aside from hatred, disappointment may be experienced by those who believe in illusion. But rarely is disillusionment experienced. Most people are like what an eastern mystic once described as dogs because as dogs sometimes eat their own vomit (gross I know) people eat their own vomitus in the form of failed relationships, sorrow of disease, unfulfillable desires, they keep looking for more relationships and having more children and trying to make more money because they reason "if only I get more I will be happy and secure"; never stopping to think that those things never made anyone happy or secure in an abiding way and in the end all of that will be lost no matter what is attained, yet they keep on trying again and again only to be disappointed again and again. In the case of Moses, Jesus, Buddha, Mohammed they were not seeking worldly attainments of happiness which are fleeting; their attention was turned towards what transcends those and so the world could not disappoint them. Or we might say they were greedy for heaven and the world cannot take what is attained in spirit, only the world.

Question:

Enjoyed your essay!!! Your statement in regards to Evangelicals belief in the origin of earth, *'this is very much like the idea promoted by present day evangelical and fanatical Christians who refuse to believe in the science of Geology which has shown by carbon dating and other means, that the world is much older than 6,000 years old.'*

Are you stating that the reason Evangelicals can't see that science proves that this world is over 6000 years old because of demons shielding the truth from them? Mainly people who are evangelical or fanatical Christians share this point of view? Just seeking clarification.

Answer by Dr. Ashby:

Thank you for your kind words. Your question is very interesting in that I have reflected further on my statements and as I do I realize that they are not based on my own interpretation of a fanatical point of view. Actually, the assertion of not believing in science comes from avowed fundamentalists as well as the statement about being tested by God. Those are statements that have been repeatedly given by fundamentalists that apparently have come to be accepted in the mainstream, perhaps because the fundamentalists want them to be and moderates do not contradict them. Whether or not it is a demon who is doing the shielding, I was drawing attention to the similarity but that is a connection that I think is logical to be made based on the literature of western culture and the statements by the orthodox, and fundamentalist ranks of western religion. Believing in forces outside of oneself that control one's actions logically leads to the idea that one's actions are caused by those forces and therefore it follows that one does not have control. I have always believed in the Russian proverb that says *"**In every joke there is a little bit of truth**.*" So Flip Wilson's one-liner is actually based on centuries old ideas which actually did not exist prior to the advent of the Judeo-Christian-Zoroastrian traditions that introduced the idea of a god and a devil as separate entities from human beings that are responsible for good or evil in the world. I would suppose that there are others who hold the same point of view that the world is not more than 6,000 years old but I do not know of any who are not followers of the conservative Judeo-Christian Biblical tradition that espouses that idea. In the end , whether they realize it or not, the consequences of actions show that human beings are responsible for their actions and that is based on their ability to follow truth or illusion, virtue or vice, etc. It is interesting to see in the stories such as the Quest for the Holy Grail how humanity operates in cycles of degradation and exaltation and in the degraded state the people need to climb again up the ladder of social discovery to evolve, by trial and error, systems of government, religion, philosophy, etc. all the while forgetting the glory of civilizations past that learned those things but which were rejected by the new and degraded culture. And just as we saw the downfall of Rome, the most technologically advanced culture of its time, what are we seeing now?

The Limits of Faith

Question:

Wow, this was a great essay! Your conclusion is so sad, but true

Answer by Dr. Ashby

Greetings, Thank you for your kind words.

I agree that from a worldly perspective it is indeed very sad and the untold human suffering is quite enormous and staggering, from the suffering of individuals to the suffering of countries. Even if we say that there are countries not at war, with no famine and with lots of wealth there is still disease, competition, unfulfilled desires and ultimately, death for everyone. Even if we entertain the idea that the truth is maligned in favor of political or religious ideologies that are irrational and that some people can discover great wealth and power we must also remember that there is always tomorrow and that things always change so that the world cannot stay the same. It cannot stay in harmony and not in misery. Yet from a philosophical point of view the changeableness and traitorousness of the world is supposed to raise questions, questions that lead to truth-seeking. Questions like, "if the world changes constantly how will I ever discover abiding happiness and security in the world?" The unsteadiness of the world should lead to enlightening questions as opposed to irrational mind-numbing, intellect atrophying religious dogmas, or political slogans. And if that were to occur, at least in the individual if not for entire societies, that would lead to freedom from illusion in those circles and if that were to spread then there would be more understanding in the world. But seldom has there been peace and harmony in the world, but always there has been peace and harmony for those who strive for, live and promote truth. I think that is the most important goal for all to strive for.

Question:

Dr. Ashby, I think I see what you are saying. Their is a path of degeneration to those who seek to attain "worldly" desires. And likewise a path of generation to those who seek spiritual goals. So the attainment of worldly desires decreases the attainment of spiritual goals. Much like a

The Limits of Faith

see-saw of desire, if you will, where the whole is divided among the two and balance is a Law.

Answer by Dr. Ashby

Greetings, I think your analogy of the "see-saw" is right on! I would add that children playing with the see-saw can do that endlessly, accomplishing nothing but the feeling of fun from the sensations of going up and down. In the same way adults play see-saw but with adult objects such as emotions, desires, illusions and thoughts based on a mixture of reality and illusion that they cannot get off of as long as they accept the illusion as the reality. The person that believes in the Hollywood or Washington or Biblical or Chivalry or Secular or Capitalist or Communist version of reality is like a child caught up in an illusion but they cannot get off the see-saw as long as the belief in the see-saw remains.

Question:

Is it possible to get off the sea-saw and onto the parallel bars? As a critical thinker I cannot help but consider there must be some connections between science and religion. I had a similar discussion with a Dean of Religion at a University and he concurred. Of course, I tend to believe this Dean came from an interfaith perspective of many paths to God. Devout Christians reflect on what Christ says in that:

Jesus answered, "I am the way and the truth and the life. No one comes to the Father except through me."

At times, I cannot help but wonder if Christ was delivering this message to a particular group of people who did not know God and needed strict guidance? Is it possible that Christ did not apply this message to those already in strong relationship with God, as in the Jewish (his chosen) people?

Does balance always have to be "law"? Cannot one be faithful while questioning or considering another perspective?

The Limits of Faith

Answer by Dr. Ashby

Greetings, many Christian scholars hold the view that statements such as these which are also found in the old testament are indeed dedicated to creating a messianic and special delineated image to follow and distinguish itself from the wilderness of other cults. Mystics interpret this statement as meaning that the way is through Christhood, i.e. Spiritual Enlightenment not that it must be through Christianity only. So Buddhists, Taoists, Native Americans African Religion practitioners, etc. can attain but it must be through that same process of enlightened consciousness.

However, naturally in a fundamentalist environment where literal interpretations and historicity are applied to all statements of the Bible the statement is related as exclusive to Jesus and thus also exclusive to Christianity and all others are out, lost, and consequently heathens going to hell, unworthy of compassion and therefore as happened with the Native Americans, open to conquest, cooptation and decimation. This is considered as the degradation of religious practice, not the ideal that was espoused by the original creators of Christianity before the Roman church councils and before the advent of orthodoxy in Christianity and the acceptance of Christianity by the Roman emperors. The alternative view of Jesus as a teacher and Christhood as a title, like Buddha or Krishna or enlightened being, is evident in the Gnostic Christian Texts that were excluded from the canon of the Bible by the orthodox Christians.

Question:

Thank you for the thoughtful response. Your question: "what are we seeing now" in comparison to the downfall of Rome is timely. In my view, the start of the 21st century began with the technology revolution in the world wide web. I believe we are seeing a change with more impact than the industrial revolution in the early 1900's. In our case today, the internet provides a global resource for every group: cultural, religious, businesses, etc. It seems that through easier access to information, other countries will gain more Western influences in their culture. Moreover, Americans may gain more understanding of other cultures, having access to first hand information (from the country itself) rather than through books written by Americans. For example, some resources (i.e. CD of the Essence of

The Limits of Faith

Bhagwat Gita - physically sold in India alone but available for purchase through the Internet directly from India).

Great question Dr. Ashby! What do you think we are seeing now?

Answer by Dr. Ashby

Though there are positive signs in people communicating through the internet, that does not seem to be translating into effective actions that influence the course of the dominant culture in the world today which seems to be acting with impunity to execute its own designs regardless of the consequences to the environment or to the needs of other countries but protecting the needs of the wealthy and powerful. Did these things not also happen to ancient Rome? Then the barbarians were waiting at the gates. With the disengagement of the dollar from the gold standard, the present devaluation of the dollar, the real estate bubble, the rise of global warming and the coming health care crisis it appears to be Rome all over again. Who are the barbarians now? Corporations? This reminds me of movies such as Robocop, and others where the corporations take over the insolvent government and the tyrants are in the board room!

The Meaning of Evanescence, Faith in Technology and "Does Science Only Improve?"

In the Arthurian Legends the character Lancelot appears now to be a metaphor of the predicament that is experienced by most human beings. An ordinary person's incapacity to pursue or even conceive of a reality beyond that which is presented by the senses places them at quite a disadvantage in the task of determining the absolute truth or reality. Thus most people are satisfied with or at least acquiesce to the basic cause and effect relationships of the mundane nature of life. Their faith is based on and limited by their limited perceptions of reality. Without a guiding philosophy or a method to extricate themselves from ordinary time and space reality they are continually bombarded with advertisements and pressures of the world defining them as limited and mortal individuals. Internally there is pressure also as human beings accept the phenomenal reality as absolute and abide by its apparent cause and effect relationships which are actually not so rigid.

Descartes' attempts to extricate himself from the pressures of the world, seeking solace in a furnace, reflects his desire to find a way to exercise pure reason or transcending the pressures of time and space, to rise above the faulty senses. Yet if the philosophy that informs that quest is itself based on time and space conceptions, then ultimately the quest is also faulty. In other words, if the idea is to extricate oneself from the world because the world is illusory then what is true? How can reality be determined? Why would extrication from the world lead to a reality and not just another illusion? That is to say, the concepts of faith or empiricism are not absolute realities; they are merely concepts, constructs of the mind, just like fullness and emptiness. Emptiness as a concept is as real as fullness since it is a construct of the mind just as a dream world in the mind of a dreaming person is as real as the waking world of a waking person. In a dream the objects that appear to be present or absent are both illusory. The experiments on physical matter by particle accelerator machines show that matter is not "real" but rather existing in a form of appearance sustained by energetic vibrations. Further, matter is 99.99%empty space and the observable aspect of matter is an image as we "know" matter is composed of atomic particles that are moving constantly. So matter is not static, though it appears to be. Therefore, the dream reality is as un-abiding as the waking reality.

John Locke (1632-1704) was an English philosopher who was concerned primarily with society and epistemology. Locke has often been classified, along with David Hume and George Berkeley, as a British Empiricist. If Locke believed in intuition (primarily as it concerned the existence of God), but all intuition, to be knowledge, had finally to be demonstrable: ". . .intuition and demonstration are the degrees of our knowledge; whatever comes short. . .no matter . . . with what assurance soever embraced, is but faith or opinion, but not knowledge. . ." then how could he have exercised such a profound influence on subsequent philosophy and politics in the 18th century. His ideas concerning liberty and the social contract later influenced the written works of Thomas Jefferson, James Madison, and other "Founding Fathers" of the United States [in particular, the Declaration of Independence- He also had a major influence on the US Constitution in the Preamble.][72] Locke had the idea that "all" men had the natural rights of life, liberty, the pursuit of happiness, and estate; ideas which may be considered quintessential ideals of the "founding fathers" of the United States of America." Locke also developed the Lockeian social contract which included the state of nature, government with the consent of the governed and all the natural rights.[73] The point is that if he was an empiricist, where did he get the ideas from? Which society did he study "empirically" to arrive at the conclusions that human beings have natural rights to life, liberty, the pursuit of happiness, and estate and that there should be a social contract between human beings and their government? The point is that those are intuitional realities. Intuitional realities may be defined as "recognized truths which escape the ordinary sense perception capacity." They are recognized not by the ordinary sense perceptions or egoistic personality but by the higher evolves sensibility that connects the innermost reality within a human being to the essence of all Creation. How do we explain love? Can love be empirically measured, yet it exists, as well as hate, desire, etc. if we say that hate, for instance, is measured by the manifestation in worldly hostility what of the hate that is not

The Limits of Faith

manifested but just harbored in the hearts of men and women. So we "know" they are there and yet there is no explanation or measure for them. Intuitional realities are not arrived at through empirical experimentation but experiences in the world of time and space lead to intuitional realizations of higher ideals and absolute truths. That is supposed to be the purpose of authentic spiritual inquiry and that concept is contained in the ancient Egyptian and ancient Greek admonition: "Know Thyself." In this sense true science would lead to intuitional realization of truth which is not empirically oriented but yet is experienced by the scientist who has now become the mystic.

The underlying philosophical idea that a person uses in the search for truth guides the person's methodologies and conclusions either in a negative or positive way. Thus, the underlying philosophical idea of assigning reality the dual nature of either faith or reason is faulty because either concept is illusory, based on time and space realities that are themselves illusory. This should mean that a-priori knowledge [gained by reason alone] is as valid as "a-posteriori" [gained through empirical means]. Both a-priori and a-posteriori "knowledge" are spurred on by sensory stimulus and the desiring nature of the mind. So whether one turns towards faith or empirical scientific experiments one is reacting to what one perceives and understands as one's relationship to physical phenomena, again, which is illusory. Therefore the assertion that knowledge either has to or does not have to be demonstrable in order to be considered knowledge or otherwise should be considered faith or opinion, is incorrect. The idea here is that conceptual knowledge precedes time and space knowledge but is constructed by interacting with physical objects in a rudimentary form of experimentation such as when a child touches a hot stove. The knowledge gained is that it is hot and hurts! Yet it is not necessary to put the hand in a burning fire to understand the reality. So understanding reality can occur via deductive reasoning or reflection based on observation as well as experience through life or scientific experimentation but also extrapolation, which is not based on observations or experiments or experiences. Even in ordinary life situations there are many "realities" that are unexplained. Food sustains life and scientists can explain some of the how but no scientist can explain why, yet it does. At a certain point food does not sustain life and no scientist can explain why; saying that a person gets old and must die is not an explanation of the reason but it is an explanation of an event and that is not the same as knowledge and yet the

The Limits of Faith

masses of society accept the limited and ignorant explanations of scientists because even though they do not have all the answers they are perceived as being closer to them than those who do not conduct experiments. However, that rationale is faulty because even though scientists have gained sufficient "knowledge" to manipulate certain physical phenomena (ex. Manipulate oil to make gasoline to run engines) that knowledge is limited and conditional, functioning only in this time and space reality and even then under certain conditions [which are not understood], which is why scientific breakthroughs and laws are not abiding, but rather conditional in their applicability. A skydiver loses the parachute and yet survived the fall to earth while another falls in the same way to his doom. How did it happen? Why did it happen? This illusoriness of so called empirical reality also "explains" why there are certain engineering and medical inventions that seem to work sometimes or most times while others fail most times but work sometimes; bridges collapse, planes crash and medicines that in the beginning seemed to be the "holy grail" of medicine later turn out to be the latest recalled drug that killed many people and was only created and allowed to get on the market to enrich drug companies. Along with the corruption of the drug industry there is the defective medical system itself, which annually kills 100,000 people due to malpractice issues and then there are those who die due to adverse drug interactions.

So we cannot say that science only improves nor can we say that science is an abiding reality as it is based on a concept that is limited to time and space which is illusory and also it studies phenomena that are illusory and changeable. So there can be no absolute experimental conclusions from time and space science activities, only limited knowledge that may help to improve life for some. Nevertheless, the knowledge gained by scientists is tainted by their own conceptions of reality. Albert Einstein took a different stance; he pursued science alongside religious faith and philosophical reflection.

- But science can only be created by those who are thoroughly imbued with the aspiration toward truth and understanding. This source of feeling, however, springs from the sphere of religion. To this there also belongs the faith in the possibility that the regulations valid for the world of existence are rational, that is, comprehensible to reason. I cannot conceive of a genuine scientist without that profound faith. The situation may be expressed by an image: **science without religion is lame, religion without science is blind.** Though I have

The Limits of Faith

asserted above that in truth a legitimate conflict between religion and science cannot exist, I must nevertheless qualify this assertion once again on an essential point, with reference to the actual content of historical religions. This qualification has to do with the concept of God. During the youthful period of mankind's spiritual evolution human fantasy created gods in man's own image, who, by the operations of their will were supposed to determine, or at any rate to influence, the phenomenal world. Man sought to alter the disposition of these gods in his own favor by means of magic and prayer. The idea of God in the religions taught at present is a sublimation of that old concept of the gods. Its anthropomorphic character is shown, for instance, by the fact that men appeal to the Divine Being in prayers and plead for the fulfillment of their wishes.

- *Science, Philosophy and Religion, A Symposium*, published by the *Conference on Science, Philosophy and Religion in Their Relation to the Democratic Way of Life, Inc.*, New York (1941)

Along with the above, Einstein said that the perception of separateness in nature is an "optical illusion." Einstein reasoned a-priori or in a higher sense, *intuitionally* that true scientific investigation cannot succeed without spiritual insight because his mind was able to conceptualize the limitations of science that must necessarily take the mind into realms of thought that are "un-provable" but are nevertheless realities. In the quote above he refers to rationality not as a means to rationalize a concept down to a simple and acceptable idea that the mind can accept as reality but as the understanding in the mind of reality as it is. In other words, faith should lead to truth as it is and not as conceptualized due to a particular view of a religious denomination or the political decrees of political leaders. He was a forerunner of the discipline of physics which came to be referred to as "quantum" which itself stretches the boundaries of ordinary scientific thought and experimentation and breaks through the rigid requirements of empirical proof.

If the relative reality of time and space indeed operates as the quantum physicists suggest: "subatomic particles do not appear to function under cause and effect relationships, nor to obey any of the laws of time-space we normally consider to be the context of all phenomena" then it follows that the very foundation upon which reality rests, the substratum of physical reality, the universe, is itself not based on quantifiable, rational, orderly laws, at least in terms of ordinary human conceptualizations. The limitation in rationalizing (in terms of Einstein's definition) observable reality renders the search for truth defective.

The Limits of Faith

Therefore the classical question of a "first cause" considered by Aristotle, Anselm, and Parmenides, and others is limited and illusory. David Hume, himself conceptualized no first cause at all, like the "Shunya" concept of Buddhism, which conceives of reality springing forth from a source-less void. If there is no cause or all comes from a void where did the phenomena come from. Saying it just "exists" is not an answer, just an explanation of the observation. If we say that "everything occurs simultaneously, as is conceived of in Chan (Zen) Buddhism, as well as other systems of Eastern thought" we are still explaining how something works and not what it is and or where it came from.

So at least in the discipline of quantum physics we are returning to the original discipline of a-priori that is informed by a transcendental philosophy of reality instead of limiting the philosophy and therefore the results of our investigation to what is "observable" "quantifiable" or "empirical." Of course this harkens back to the days of mystics and transcendental philosophies which beckon our return to the source of reality which is beyond the mind, beyond physical phenomena, beyond our egoistic concepts, our politics and our religious myths. And if we were to strip ourselves from those limiting concepts what would be left. That is the unspoken name, the reality that can be experience but not qualified. So we should not complain to mystics that they cannot explain reality to us for it would be like a quantum physicist attempting to explain quantum physics to ants and roaches. The ants and roaches experience a different reality and their capacity to understand is bound by their limited intellects and capacity to transcend the limitations of their minds. But lest we should think that understanding reality is about higher use of mind; it is about transcending mind itself and even the concept of transcending the mind itself since "transcending the mind itself" is also a concept as is language. Therefore, the concepts must stop and the speech must stop and the writing must stop so at some point that the intuition may take flight…

Question:

Dr. Ashby, Couldn't the intuition of a mystic be as faulty as any demonstrable proof science may offer? The descriptions of mystical intuitions appear to differ from one another. Is this only the problem of the limitations of language or is every (or most) intuited reality unique? It

The Limits of Faith

seems to be difficult to know absolutely what another human (or ant) has experienced or knows.

Answer by Dr. Ashby

Sometimes people who are considered mystics are in reality having ecstatic experiences, mingled with ecstasy and emotion or perhaps delusion or even mental illness. In the sense of mysticism as espoused in recognized mystical texts such as Vedanta of India or the Per M Hru of Africa, the Tao of China, etc. mysticism is transcending time and space references and concepts into the real of substratum which is common ground for all mystics regardless of their religious tradition. To me the descriptions offered in those texts as well as in the writings of some Sufis and Christian mystics such as Teresa De Avila reflect a remarkable similarity and therefore a common basis for what is termed Absolute.

Science, Faith or The Transcendental? The Debate over Creationism or Evolution and other Related Issues.

In the book, *Red Giants and White Dwarfs,* by Robert Jastrow, the author presents scientific discoveries that were amazing testaments to human ingenuity and technological advancement. However, they were also more pressure that upset many who were not ready to agree that the world was billions of years old (Jastrow, Ch. 9) instead of the thousands that the Biblical tradition had instructed. As a student of world mythology I have noticed that the Western theologians have a tougher time reconciling the discoveries of science as opposed to the Eastern ones. The Western monotheistic ones seem committed to a concrete and unchanging picture of reality, which probably comes from the tradition of seeing religion as a historical as opposed to metaphorical discipline of spiritual development. Such a view would necessarily be at odds with anything that seems to contradict its certain view of reality. On the other hand, religions from pantheistic or henotheistic religions would seem to flexible enough to incorporate the new discoveries into themselves without much disruption. For example, the Ancient Egyptian religion has a teaching of Creation that ascribes the age of Creation on the order of "millions and millions" of years. So it would not be difficult to reconcile that with the modern scientific understanding. In the East and in Africa as well as Native American religions the new discoveries might even seem to confirm the teachings of those ancient traditions.

The Genesis account of Creation, along with the Creation Myth of other religious traditions, from which it seemed to arise, would seem to be at odds with the Big Bang theory. The Creation myth holds that Creation arose from a stirring of primeval waters. If those waters could be seen as the primordial soup (chapter 11, amino acids, etc) of undifferentiated matter that was produced originally, perhaps we might be able to say that that soup was the leftover or aftermath from the Big Bang. But one cosmology suggests calm creation out of what was there previously and the other a violent explosion into the realm of time and space that continues rushing outward from who knows where to where knows who.

Rationality would seem to demand that we should adopt a new truth when we recognize it as such. The Dalai Lama, a world leader of Buddhism, has said that if a scientific discovery contradicts Buddhist teachings that the Buddhist teachings should accept that new reality. Could we imagine a leader of any of the Western religions making such a statement even though Jesus appears to have meant the same thing in John 10 37:38? The trouble is that ordinary human consciousness has never been completely rational or capable of following truth to the explosion of the egoistic desires or fears or other weaknesses; but also, the world has never been completely predictable or fathomable either. So it would seem that those who claim absolute creationism are as deficient in their ability to arrive at a certain reality as those who claim a scientific reality. It seems that there is constant need of revising theories when new discoveries are made; That would be the definition of uncertainty or error, the necessity to make revisions; for only that which is without need of revision can be considered certain or true in an absolute sense. Yet the world seems to be full of relative truths that many scientists as well as theologians are prepared to believe now regardless of their failings. Perhaps the problem is faith in the ever-changing physical reality itself and lack of searching in places where there are no changes that confuse the mind.

John 10

[37]If I don't do the works of my Father, don't believe me. [38]But if I do them, though you don't believe me, believe the works; that you may know and believe that the Father is in me, and I in the Father."

In the Bible book of John 10 37:38, Jesus instructs that the people should believe if they have the proof of his miracles. This would mean that they should have proof in exchange for their belief, not faith, for if they have proof there would be no need for faith anymore. Thus there is a point where faith is not enough and where true belief must dawn. But here we have another conundrum; where is the proof today? Where are Jesus' miracles to convince people in the present? In the absence of Jesus or Moses or Muhammad, people seek to believe that what happened in the

The Limits of Faith

past was true literally back then and that therefore makes it true literally today also. Yet that logic is flawed because we do not have any proof that any miracle or any history of the Bible ever occurred in a literal way. Thus, that factor must be overlooked in order to proceed with the religions; thus the religion cannot pass beyond the level of faith to belief and experience. The true path to prove the past is to follow the instructions that the sages of the past handed down. If they are authentic the result should be a replication of the success of the past, the attainment of higher consciousness. But in order for that to happen people must live the life as it was outlined and not just with words, asserting one's faith. For example, Jesus professed turning the other cheek when wronged by others. How many nuclear weapons would Jesus create and use on others? How many countries would Jesus command to be invaded and millions killed to promote imperialism, corporate profits or expanding the church? This is the limit of Faith as a religious practice. Faith must be outgrown in order to have a true and viable and abiding religious experience.

Faux debate of creationism or evolution

There are many Christians who would like to have Creationism taught along side Evolution. Those who would like to promote the idea of Creationism or "Intelligent Design" would like to frame the argument as equivalent options to be chosen. Creationism is Religion and Evolution is science. The argument is nonexistent since to have a debate you would need to have equal elements to compare. In other words, to debate about whether evolution should be taught versus some other discipline, that discipline would need to be a science and not a religion. Likewise, if there were a choice between Christianity and some other philosophy that philosophy would need to be a religion and not a science.

Questions:

It seems that the more philosophical we become the less we are able to access higher consciousness and perhaps the aboriginals of the world are the chosen few?
I was wondering about your statements from the essay: "only that which is without need of revision can be considered certain or true in an absolute sense" an allegorical depiction of God the Creator and that "searching in places where there are no changes that confuse the mind" would be

The Limits of Faith

Heaven, the highest level of perfection and that "training of the higher sense" not only depicts a disciplined intuition in communion with nature but an earnest conscious beseeching, a prayer, to be in the presence of God.

Answer by Dr. Ashby,

It seems that the more philosophical we become the less we are able to access higher consciousness and perhaps the aboriginals of the world are the chosen few?

I would not see the aboriginals as being the only chosen ones. But I think that the "aboriginal" way of looking at the world would facilitate our ability to transcend into other realms of awareness that the technologized cultured world has tended to dismiss. And we can recapture that wherever we are if we look at the world correctly and do not get lost in the world, keeping the proper balance. The mystic philosophers and the ancient scriptures have held that all human beings (Native Americans, Europeans, Africans, Easterners, etc.) have the latent capacity. It is simply dormant when the personality concentrates on worldly pursuits instead of mystic research through introspection, philosophy and meditation. Genetically, the people of the technologically advanced societies are no different from the aboriginal ones. So the same capacity is there in both.

Is the statement " only that which is without need of revision can be considered certain or true in an absolute sense" an allegorical depiction of God the Creator?

I think that in terms of a person seeking certainty in life they would seek something that would appear to be perfect in terms of not apparently needing revision or projecting on it, investing in it such a status. It would follow that if they are seeking a perfect God that God concept and its attendant teaching should need no revisions for if it did it would lose the status of certain and therefore also the status of real since their conception of reality is bound up in the concept of certainty.

And the statement that "searching in places where there are no changes that confuse the mind" would be Heaven, the highest level of perfection?

The Limits of Faith

Heaven is differently defined in different spiritual traditions. In African and Eastern thought it is a place of temporary residence where one experiences the fruits of one's good karma {good deeds} but one comes back when the experience is over, to the world to be reincarnated. In the West it is a place to reside with God in happiness forever. In relative terms heaven can be experienced while on earth as in the after death state, according to the mystic philosophy, based on ones level of consciousness or level of self-knowledge. Therefore, in worldly terms the search for simple dogmas in order to ease the mental burden is not heaven in a religious or philosophical way of thought. Most people want mental peace and when there is strife in life the easiest way to seek that is pushing away hard or complicated theories or spiritual disciplines and adopting simple ones. The mystic strives for simplicity but simplicity is not confused with dogma and blind faith; simplicity means absence of complication and entanglement with egoism and worldly desires; it is that which complicates life, colors the perception of self and reality and atrophies the intellect- so a person is rendered incapable of understanding the mystic philosophy and so gravitates to simple dogmas. Many people say "ignorance is bliss" but in the end the ignorance turns into shock, like smoking is dangerous to health; the blissful ignorance is not facing that or pushing that understanding aside and enjoying the smoke, but the rude awakening from that bliss is cancer and painful death. That is the worldly ignorance and if you will, the worldly heaven, which is sweet in the beginning and bitter in the end or as Lord Krishna would say, "nectar in the beginning and poison in the end." That is not perfection but an illusion based on worldly desires.

And the statement that "training of the higher sense" not only depicts a disciplined intuition in communion with nature but an earnest conscious beseeching, a prayer, to be in the presence of God?

Yes I think this is right on in terms of the philosophy; those disciplines which allow the higher perception are dynamic and powerful entreaties but more than that, qualifications to assume the innate position we already hold. For that communion with nature is already there, we are already part of nature; this week we breathe the air that the Chinese people breathed last week and next week they will breathe ours; today we eat chlorophyll in salad that plants transformed sunlight into; this year we pass through, on space ship earth, a part of the galaxy that other stars passed and perhaps other living beings on other spaceship earths, years ago or perhaps even now on another dimension; it is fascinating and dare I say, even glorious. For if what the quantum physicists and the mystics say is true, then we need not look to far or pray too hard since we are already in the presence of the Supreme.

Questions:

The truth sometimes changes over time, based on experience/life/lessons learned/knowledge etc. The Book of Genesis (or even the Bible as a whole) if not taken literally, can really show some similarities to what we find or have discovered through science.

Answer by Dr. Ashby:

One of your statements fascinated me since I have studied its meaning for many years. You said that if the Bible book of Genesis is "not taken literally". That is a central point in our study because the very conservative faith-based community says it should be considered as literal, while moderate believers in the Bible are more flexible and mystics even from Hinduism or Buddhism would find some commonality. Perhaps even the Quantum Physicists could agree; But as long as the Bible must be seen as absolutely certain and literal and historical, to the exclusion of other cultures, philosophies or traditions, that confluence of ideas would not be possible.

One of the most important problems of faith as a method of knowing is that it can be easily used as a means to overlook or ignore contradictions. For example, there is no evidence outside the Bible that a Jewish exodus out of Egypt occurred. Also, in Jesus' time there are no records of his existence or his deeds outside of the Bible. In contrast, the Ancient Egyptian religion speaks of the personality Asar (Osiris). We can find historical records in other cultures of that time acknowledging the existence of Asar and we can find Asarian temples of that time in Egypt and other countries. The earliest writings related to Jesus occur in the Gospel books of the Christian Bible, after the destruction of the Jewish temple. Since we know that the destruction that is mentioned in the Gospels occurred at or after the year 70 C.E., that indicates the writings occurred 70 years after Jesus was supposedly alive. Furthermore, none of

The Limits of Faith

the versions of the gospels agree with the others or with the varied versions of themselves. So the writings appear to have come from different sources, none of which was directly associated with the supposedly historical Jesus. Yet, even though Christology scholars know the aforementioned facts and many others, most of them, along with Christian theologians still advocate faith in the historical Jesus by affirming faith while alluding to the mysterious ways of God's scriptures, thereby admonishing followers to suspend rational thought processes in favor of blind acceptance of patently contradictory theological ideas. So it is more important to believe in Jesus as a real historical personality than to examine critically the errors of the Bible; instead the errors are masked through an all-encompassing concept that the "whole Bible" is the "word of God" and must therefore be accepted in its entirety, without questioning its contradictions. This is not to say that Christianity is devoid of value. The point is that the historical argument is false. If it were possible to leave the historicity if religion behind it might be possible to discover the deeper principles of the religion that are stifled by the effort to affirm historicity and superiority.

Question:

About the ancients who wrote the Bible, perhaps we should be contented with the understanding that some things just can't be explained (or maybe they can but it is beyond our concept or grasp of understanding) so they worked with what they had, based on their knowledge.

Answer by Dr. Ashby:

Again, I see your point, but if some things cannot be explained, what hope is there for arriving at true understanding? This is a dilemma that forced the move towards faith-based certain and literal interpretations. Also, if they worked with what they had would that not mean that we have more advanced understanding because we supposedly "have" more? Yet we see that the world is not so benefited by the more that we supposedly have. Our technology is increased but greed and misunderstanding have also.

But more importantly, if they only "worked with what they had" would that not mean that they were limited and therefore what they did cannot be considered certain or final? What value would it have then? These are

The Limits of Faith

conundrums that it is great for us to discuss because these, I believe, are issues that are driving much human interaction in the world today.

What the ancients did has value if they worked to discover the universal principles that transcend time, that is, the principles of life that apply to people in the past, present and future. Then there would be no need for revisions. If we try to interpret an absolute truth literally we will always fail because the relative reality of the world will always change. So what is real yesterday, today and tomorrow? That is the important question. If we dedicate ourselves to that and not try to appropriate the answer by saying "our group has the absolute truth and everyone else is wrong" then we will there is a chance to discover the transcendental mysteries of life. Otherwise only limitation and objects or philosophies of contention will be discovered.

Question:

While I understand the need to have proof to justify the science, I have to interject that for someone to believe in Creationism, you also have to possess a measure of faith. To many who possess a deep faith in God, they will argue with you regarding being able to feel Him. For those who might not have ever experienced that or do not share that in your personal faith, it might be hard to relate. That person would say that you might not be able to see God, but you can't see the wind either. What you do witness is the effect that the wind has. The same is true for God. You can see His effect on the person and thus if you believe He created the Universe, you can see the effect He had on Creation.

Answer by Dr. Ashby:

Thank you for this discourse. However I am not sure of the analogies here. This is the problem in relating science and religion – they are hard to relate philosophically or theoretically. Science is based on a scientific method and religion is based on myth so the scientific method cannot be applied to religion unless the religion is based on a scientific theory. This is why scientists point out that Creationism cannot be taught as a science. Saying that God is the cause behind something as an article of faith cannot be studied scientifically because there is no God to observe. However,

The Limits of Faith

wind, like atoms, can be studied because they can be captured, manipulated, measured, etc., even though they may cannot be seen, they can be perceived.

If a religion is based on a scientific theory then that can be studied scientifically because the result of the scientific religion can be measured. For example, in the Dhammapada text of Buddhism it is directed that an aspirant should not believe in the scripture but in experience. So if the eight-fold path that Buddha laid out were followed, the changes or lack of changes in the aspirant could be studied and measured and a determination could be made if changes arose from the practices enjoined. If Nirvana were the result of the Buddhist practices the spiritual technology (eight-fold path) was the effective cause and the Buddha Consciousness (i.e. God) that arose was the underlying cause. If there is only faith and if the resolution is that things cannot be known because they are unfathomable mysteries, then would there be any possibility for change, self-knowledge discovery or application of the scientific method to such a tradition? It would seem that that is an Agnostic position, that God exists but cannot be known with the meager human capacities? Whatever claims were made of discovery or "feeling God" through faith might be considered by others as a psychological delusion or emotional exuberance, just as one can feel deeply in a dream and yet the dream is not real. The Eastern and African or mystic view would be called Gnostic (opposite of Agnostic), that the mysteries of life can be uncovered definitively. The Christian Gnostic Gospels would agree with the mystics and would also include the theistic point of view (There is a God) but would not agree with the idea of unresolved faith (there are unfathomable mysteries that will never be understood). However, the Orthodox Church seems to reject the Gnostic Christian view, even though it developed at the same time. The Gnostic mystic, like the Eastern mystic, would see revelation coming from communion, that is, becoming one with God. The Orthodox would reject that idea, having faith in a life after physical death in the presence of God, in heaven. Sometimes there seems to be some contradiction in the writings of the Bible. The writings of the Bible may lead us to questions such as "is God a transcendental mystery, or is God revealed in flesh?" (**Paul's First Letter to Timothy 3: 16**) And "how is God to be known, in flesh as Jesus, in Spirit as the Father, or in the Heart, wherein is the Kingdom of Heaven or Christ Consciousness?" I recall the words of the Bible which speak of the mystery of God but also the words which speak of discovery (**Luke

The Limits of Faith

Chapter 8, 15-18). These questions, the introspection they engender and the actions we take based on these deliberations are great issues that humanity has been struggling with especially since the advent of the Western religions. They are also important to our present and future development and relations on earth and how we search for meaning in life. Much confusion has arisen out of the scriptures and most people deal with the problem by relying on faith. But faith cannot answer conundrums that are based on erroneous premises and flawed logic.

Paul's First Letter to Timothy 3: 16

[16] Without controversy, the mystery of godliness is great:
> God was revealed in the flesh,
> justified in the spirit,
> seen by angels,
> preached among the nations,
> believed on in the world,
> and received up in glory.

Luke Chapter 8, 15-18

[15] That in the good ground, these are such as in an honest and good heart, having heard the word, hold it tightly, and bring forth fruit with patience.
[16] "No one, when he has lit a lamp, covers it with a container, or puts it under a bed; but puts it on a stand, that those who enter in may see the light. [17] For nothing is hidden, that will not be revealed; nor anything secret, that will not be known and come to light. [18] Be careful therefore how you hear. For whoever has, to him will be given; and whoever doesn't have, from him will be taken away even that which he thinks he has."

The Limits of Faith

Question:

You said previously:

"I agree that the "universe could actually be a projection of the consciousness of God but I also do believe that it is an actual and physical reality as there are empirically measurable results in its exploration, most likely due to its existence as "a projection of quantum events or strings, etc."

I find it hard to perceive that the impetus for such polar creative/destructive forces and universal energies originates within each of us and emanates from our relatively limited capacities. That concept seems somewhat hedonistic and anthropocentric to me. … what we experience before and after we have entered this life in our present fleshly form… In that, the Kingdom of Heaven is most certainly beyond and not within us... but what IS within us is the spiritual "genome", the building blocks of a spiritual life...the primordial soup beyond the plane of our reality... "Living Water" if you will...enabled by the "spoken Word of God"...indeed calling us out as the composite of quantum particles that we are...differentiated and undifferentiated drops in an unseen primeaval ocean. And that, I believe, is how our outside intention can affect the behaviour of quantum particles in a "God" definition...and the simplest proof is the test of FAITH!"

Answer by Dr. Ashby

Your ideas recalled to mind the writings from Ancient Egypt called *Memphite Theology* and another set called the *Harper's Songs*. In Memphite Theology, the God Ptah brought Creation into being by speaking neteru or gods and goddesses (cosmic forces) into being that took the shape of the physical reality by forming matter into the shapes that their particular energetic mission that was directed by Ptah caused them to take on. The Harper's writings extol the beauty of the world but nevertheless instruct that the earthly existence is fleeting and dreamlike and therefore one should prepare for a higher reality.

The Limits of Faith

I have heard these songs
which are in the ancient tombs,
which tell of the virtues of life on earth
and make little of life in the Neterchert (cemetery).
Why then do likewise to eternity?
It is a place of justice, without fear,
where uproar is forbidden,
where no one attacks his fellow.
This place has no enemies;
all our relatives have lived in it from time immemorial,
with millions more to come.
It is not possible to linger in Egypt –(on earth)
no one can escape from going west (end of life- Netherworld).
One's acts on earth are like a dream.
'Welcome safe and sound!'
to who ever arrives in the West.

-Ancient Egyptian Harper's Song

In contrast, I do not find it hard to believe that we are as projections on the stage of the grand canvas that would be the universe. If we consider that when we sleep we are actually projecting reality within our minds that is as "solid" and real and "fleshy" as any waking experience it is not so hard to conceptualize. Should we say that the dream world is as real as the waking world? Conversely, should we say that the waking world is no more real than the dream world? And what about the dreamless sleep state? What happens when there is neither dream nor waking but there is something nevertheless? The philosophy thus holds that none of these realities are "real" or abiding and what is real is what sustains all the three states of consciousness. In accordance with the philosophy, if one were to discover that substratum, which is beyond matter including dark matter, then one would discover the source of all sources, the Supreme Being. That would be an internal discovery, meaning that it is discovered to be the essence of the self in all things, the stars, the planets, the animals, the plants and the human mind or shall we say transcending that mind to its essential nature. Therefore, from the perspective of this non-Western philosophy, considering that the observations of the waking, dream and dreamless deep sleep by the sages are corroborated by the instability of the three states and the scientific findings that matter is composed of star material that was formed when stars exploded and through entropy therefore will some day go back to its original state (undifferentiated), as well as the findings that matter exists across different domains (solid (and invisible- proven by indirect experiments,[i] energy (proven by Einstein), nothing (proven by particle accelerator experiments) means that none of the states of consciousness nor the states of matter are abiding and therefore also not real, it would follow that the faith in the idea of the universe and the physical body as abiding and solid realities would seem to me to be the hedonistic and anthropocentric conception because it believe in and relies on the body the physical matter and the material experiences for its criterion of existence, i.e. reality. (pardon the long sentence). For the mystical philosophy does not see the body or the universe as abiding; therefore it is not anthropocentric but rather *transcentric,* if I may coin the term, because it centers around the transcendental reality and not the relative reality.

If we say that we have a primordial "genome" within us from which sprouts the personality and the body and the world, like Jesus' mustard seed (Bible Matthew 13 31:32)[ii], then we might tend to see the world as a reality sprouted from our essence which would be closer to the abiding reality as in our dreams. But the reality created by a human mind in any state of consciousness is fleeting so our spiritual "genome" would be limited, prone to error, inconsistency and contradictions and therefore would not meet the criteria for something real, that is to say, abiding. Yet, if we say that the Kingdom of God is beyond us why did Jesus say the Kingdom was within us (Luke 17:20-21)[iii]? What is this kingdom "within" or maybe a better question is "what" is "IT" itself? According to the philosophy it is in our higher self, the self that is the ocean or the Spirit, i.e. Supreme Being, instead of the little self that is the drop or the soul. So in the discovery of the higher Self the limitations of the individual are transcended but since the reality of the individual is as relative as the individual the physical reality is also discovered to be illusory and therefore transcended.

---

[i] *God and the Astronomers* by Robert Jastrow, Chap 8

[ii] He set another parable before them, saying, "The Kingdom of Heaven is like a grain of mustard seed, which a man took, and sowed in his field; ³²which indeed is smaller than all seeds. But when it is grown, it is greater than the herbs, and becomes a tree, so that the birds of the air come and lodge in its branches."

[iii] Being asked by the Pharisees when the Kingdom of God would come, he answered them, "The Kingdom of God doesn't come with observation; ²¹neither will they say, 'Look, here!' or, 'Look, there!' for behold, the Kingdom of God is within you."

The Limits of Faith

The belief in the physical world and body as abiding realities is negated by life itself, which is fleeting and insecure – all things change and die and there is no secure situation or consistency anywhere. If we are to believe that the universe was produced *ex-nihilist*[i], we would be forced to assume a magical or unexplainable existence out of naught, zero, zilch. Yet the conception of the universe as a dream does not imply nothing in terms of absence of existence but rather the absence of "things" as in no-thing-ness; in other words the substance is there originally and always was there but it was unformed, undifferentiated. Creation is differentiation and the end of Creation is a return to the undifferentiated state but not the end of existence, only the end of time and space as we perceive them but not reality as God perceives it. So, while all things change and die and there is no secure situation or consistency anywhere there is something that is abiding, the perception of the changes themselves. The subject who is doing the perceiving is always the same even though caught up in different perceptions of reality (waking, dream or deem sleep or birth, youth, adulthood and old age and death.) and that is the place to discover that which is abiding and real.

However, can we say where our consciousness is? If we say that our consciousness is an excretion of the matter that composes our bodies that comes into existence, say when a sperm and an egg come together, would that not be an anthropocentric idea? But would it not be a false one since we would not be able to find where our consciousness resides in it. In other words where is the mind, in the brain, the leg, the heart? People have received transplant or have had those parts amputated and yet life and consciousness remains. Some people have had legs, arms, organs, etc. removed, and even hearts replaced or half the brain removed and they continued to remain conscious. If there is a soul, it was not in those parts. Thus, also if there is a God, which part of the Universe does He or She reside in? In a dream which part of the dream do we reside in as the creators of the dream? The philosophical answer and the answer that is discovered upon realizing the higher consciousness through meditation and other disciplines enjoined by the sages is that the dream is a projection from the source that is the abiding reality. The source is not the dream in the sense that it does not suffer the fate of the dream except in an illusory

---

[i] *God and the Astronomers* by Robert Jastrow, *The Theological Impact of the new Cosmology*

The Limits of Faith

way when the source believes it is actually in the dream experiencing the dream world- and in that delusion the pain or happiness of the dream is believed to be real. The dream is apparently real but actually fleeting and mortal but the source is abiding and immortal like a person who dreams but wakes up from the dream. So too a person who practices the philosophy can wake up from the relative dream of the waking, dream and dreamless sleep states and thus transcend the physical reality altogether. So the source projected the illusion and "resides" in it like a person experiences a television show, a reality projected from the TV studio that manifests in the home entertainment center. The studio is the source and the show is the illusion the dream and the watcher is also the source, experiencing its own Creation.

The anthropomorphic manifestation of individual consciousness is a polar manifestation of the source in the form of a microcosmic relative reality. The universe is therefore the macrocosmic opposite. But both are manifestations of the source, the Spirit, Consciousness, i.e. God, but not as anthropomorphic being but as transcendental essence, which the famed scholar Joseph Campbell would define as:

> "God is a metaphor for a mystery that transcends all human categories of thought...It depends on how much you want to think about it, whether or not it's doing you any good, whether it's putting you in touch with the mystery which is the ground of your own being."
>
> —Joseph Campbell

The universe appears to exist as solid matter because it impacts on the physical senses both in the waking and in the dream states, but it is always changing and some matter passes into energy and then into "nothingness" and then back again; the matter that passed away still exists even though the senses can no longer perceive it. So the senses are unreliable instruments to discern abiding reality and people therefore rely on the relative reality for their conclusions about existence, which will lead to erroneous assumptions, inferences and hypotheses. Where does God reside in the universe, in the matter or the "empty" space or on the other side of the galaxy? Like the microcosmic dream-world of the human mind the Universe is God's macrocosmic mental manifestation and therefore as we reside in every part of our dream so too God resides in every part of the Universe, including our cells, our feelings, our desires and our souls. But

The Limits of Faith

having a temporary residence does not mean having an abiding abode. This is why things change, suns explode, galaxies come in and out of existence and people are born and then die, because they do not belong to the world i.e. Creation, but rather are only visitors to it.

The philosophy of the universe as being like a dream does not negate its existence but relegates that existence to the position of illusory and therefore we may then move towards what is real. If we set out to study the universe as something abiding then we need to discover and prove all of its intricacies. Can we discover and prove the intricacies of even the simplest dream or the simplest waking desire or the mystery of dreamless sleep? If they are not abiding realties why would we? The pursuit of such questions as the flatness of the universe or the inflation of the universe[i] and other questions are not therefore, to learn about an abiding reality but to learn about a manifested relative reality.

It is interesting to note that the conceptions of the universe and existence in the West are strongly influenced by the philosophical concepts of *orthodoxy* in Christianity or *orthopraxis* in Judaism.[ii] The Jewish concept is not so concerned with fundamentalism so it can more readily accept or ignore the discoveries of science while the Christian orthodoxy, being *religion emphasizing correct beliefs,* ("without need of revision in an absolute sense.") must necessarily be at odds with seemingly contradictory doctrines of other religions as well as of other philosophies. Yet, if we are able to see other philosophies as means to expand our conceptions we may discover new ways to look at reality or the way to discover reality. Therefore, it will be fruitful to compare the philosophical scriptures of Ancient Egypt and India with the Western scientific and religious philosophies. In doing so there are several important insights we may gain by understanding a different perspective and way of seeking for the answers to the important questions of life.

> "After the millions of years of differentiated creation, the chaos that existed before creation will return; only the primeval god[iii] and Asar will remain steadfast-no longer separated in space and time."
> –Ancient Egyptian *Coffin Texts*

The passage above concisely expresses the powerful teaching that all creation is perishable and that even the gods and goddesses will ultimately dissolve into the primordial state of potential consciousness. Therefore, it behooves a human being to move towards the source of Creation since that is the only stable truth that exists as

---

[i] *God and the Astronomers* by Robert Jastrow, Chap 7
[ii] *God and the Astronomers* by Robert Jastrow, *Judaism, God and the Astronomers*
[iii] Referring to the Supreme Being in the form of Atum-Ra

The Limits of Faith

an abiding reality. This is known as the Absolute, from which all has emanated and into which all will dissolve. *Tm* (Tem, Tum, Atum, Atum-Ra) is the Ancient Egyptian Absolute, from which Creation arises and into which Creation will dissolve. The same transcendental and non-dualist philosophy evident in the passage above from the *Coffin Texts* can be found in the Indian *Upanishads*.

> "Before creation came into existence, Brahman (the Absolute) existed as the Unmanifest. From the Unmanifest was created the manifest. From himself he brought forth himself. Hence he is known as the Self-Existent."
> —Taittiriya Upanishad (India)

The Ancient Egyptian concept of Nun (Primeval Waters –undifferentiated consciousness) is powerfully expressed in the following passage from the *Coffin Texts*.

> "I am Nu, The Only One, without equal and I came into being at the time of my flood...I originated in the primeval void. I brought my body into existence through my own potency. I made myself and formed myself in accordance with my own desire. That which emanated from me was under my control."
> –Ancient Egyptian *Coffin Texts*

The person who practices the study, reflection and meditation upon these teachings is to discover that the Divine Self is the substratum of manifest creation and that {his/her} deeper essence and the deeper essence of all humanity is that same Self-existent Divinity which brought the entire creation into being by the power of her own will and desire. Nun is an aspect of Tem. In this aspect, it is to be understood as a formless potential matter which can convert itself into any form and any element (earth, water, fire, metal, etc.). This process may be likened to how temperature affects water. For example, very cold water becomes ice, and ice can have any shape. When very hot, the water evaporates and becomes so subtle (vapor) as to be "unmanifest." At room temperature, the same water is visible but formless. All matter is like the water. All matter is composed of the same essence which takes on the form of various objects, just as clay can take many forms. However, the forms are not abiding but temporary. God has assumed the forms of Creation just as an actor assumes a part in a play. When the play is over, the actor's mask is stripped away and the true essence of the actor's identity is revealed, just as ice melts to reveal water. The Divine Self is the substratum of all that is manifest. The same philosophy, and using almost the same exact language, is evident in the Indian *Upanishads*.

> "...In the beginning there was Existence alone—One only, without a second. He, the One, thought to himself: Let me be many, let me grow forth. Thus, out of himself he projected the universe; and having projected the universe out of himself he entered into every being."
> —Chandogya Upanishad (India)

The Limits of Faith

Question:

I know that my responses have not been necessarily taken seriously because I do not quote the Bible. Not really what I considered this conversation would truly be about. Yes, I was raised Catholic and believe in God. I was also raised in a household that gave me the option to question and have an open mind about other possibilities. Another professor pointed out to me the other day that religions are man made. All religions have been founded by man and the written word- was written by man with what proof? We are not just talking about the "one true religion" but all of the religions and their corresponding philosophies.

If we can accept the concept of God why can we not accept the paradigms of the scientific creation of the universe?

Greetings,

Indeed the discussions have not turned out the way I expected either but I think it is perhaps a factor of the world situation we have now, crises in ecology, politics, economics and religion. The topic of how we know what we know also necessarily has to involve religion since that is a primary way of people knowing or at least knowing what they think they know. And to many people, what the leaders think they know has led the world to the serious danger of cessation of all knowing. As to your question about *If we can accept the concept of God why can we not accept the paradigms of the scientific creation of the universe?* I would reflect that only those who cannot allow other ideas, that is to say, the orthodox, in any culture, cannot allow other paradigms to coexist since those would be seen as a challenge to the orthodox dogmatic conception of reality. However, scientists and atheists can be orthodox as well. There are perhaps many sources of orthodoxy but perhaps none is more dangerous than the moral fundamentalist because that characterization of the orthodoxy into moral terms reduces all to fundamental right or wrong terms like "the world is exactly this and not that" or questions like "are you with me or against me" and the world seems to be more complex than fundamental dogmas would allow. Yet no matter how much the world (universe) is complexed (if I can coin the term) it also seems to be illusory and therefore our orthodox or heterodox or ecumenical ideals are all ultimately illusory and therefore misleading us from the deeper questions of life. Religion is supposed to be a pathway to discover reunion (*relegare*- Latin, to rejoin) the soul with the Divine, just as science is

The Limits of Faith

supposed to be a window on the nature of reality. But with our over-technological world of human activity the purpose of religion and science would seem to be lost for those who seek to ignore scientific evidences while asserting dogmas, while others seek to control the world's resources or others break the boundaries of science while mindlessly bringing technologies into the world for immature human beings to use, like giving matches to children. Nevertheless, if the philosophy of quantum physics or the philosophy of mysticism are correct we may be comforted in knowing that whether or not there is a Hubble's Law[i] or a Primordial Fireball[ii] does not matter for those are things we can perhaps know in relative terms but we can also strive to go beyond that, to know who is the "knower". Then we may not need orthodoxy and perhaps we may live in peace.

Indeed all religions have been created by human beings but not all religions have been inspired by correct religious insight and intent. Some religions have been inspired by political reasons, so that one people can take the land of others, or by paranoid delusions about an impending Armageddon, and so on. Full Religion has three steps or stages, *Myth, Ritual and Mysticism.* All religions have myth that tell the story of the religion and relate the followers to the divinities of the religions. Most religions have some rituals but if they do not have mysticism, the philosophy and disciplines that allow one to actually experience the Divine (however conceived in the particular religion), then that religion will be limited; then the religion will become dogmatic and orthodox and will have conflicts with other people's myths and rituals and compete for which religion is more "true," based on myths which in the end do not lead one to true insight. The myths are only introductions to religion and are made effective through the practice of rituals when the philosophy is understood and practiced; when the personality is taken beyond the phenomenal, beyond the mundane, petty human existence. When that happens the mystics of any religion discover the same ultimate reality, not by scriptures or words but through the common experience that they lead to. The mystics therefore have no contradictions or squabbles with each other. The problem with the orthodox religions is that they are led by people who have faith but no true experiential insight into the ultimate

---

[i] *God and the Astronomers* by Robert Jastrow, Chap 4
[ii] *God and the Astronomers* by Robert Jastrow, Chap 5

The Limits of Faith

goal of religion so they lead in a limited way, through competition and conflict so as to make their traditions survive and to elevate them above others.

Question:

Previously you spoke about:

an Agnostic position, that God exists but cannot be known with the meager human capacities

This seems to me to be the dilemma I feel in the Book of Job, that after all is said and done, God's answer to Job is "Who is this that darkens my counsel without knowledge" (38:2) and Job confers (42:3) "Surely I spoke of things I did not understand, things too wonderful for me to know." This attitude of humility and self deprecation ("42:6 -I despise myself and repent in dust and ashes" is a theme in Judeo-Christian, and yet....reviewing all these scientific theories has me thinking, this is too wonderful for me to know. It is mind boggling to grasp the enormity of what we are studying. That is my viewpoint from an "average" person and perhaps that is why scientists (and doctors) are bestowed an almost "godly" authority in that they can understand these things.

Answer by Dr. Ashby

I see where you're coming from. Especially after reading the books in the course so far it certainly seems daunting and that is just related to the scientific knowledge! What of the knowledge of the religious scriptures not just of the Judeo-Christian Bible but what of the Hindu Bible, the Ancient Egyptian Bible, the Buddhist Bible, etc.! I also think about the giants of science like Einstein and as I was growing up I was awed by them and the great spiritual teachers like Jesus. Osiris, Isis, Krishna, Kwan Yin and Buddha but I also realized that their myths all relate to the ordinary human. They were all weak and feeble human beings when they began their journey and they all rose up by inquiring and working towards self-knowledge. They all imparted the teaching that we can all do the same because we are made of the same stuff as they were; we may even have some of the same atoms that were in their bodies! Therefore we have the same potential. We already have the spark, the seed, and all it needs is nurturing, proper kindling, the sun and rain of proper truth seeking and that is the real dilemma, how to properly seek the truth. We have the capacity and the ancients have shown the way; and that way is confirmed,

The Limits of Faith

not negated by science. This to me is a most heartening affirmation from the ancients to us and those who will come after (if there is an after). Therefore I prefer the Gnostic position, that we can know. All the evidences of mystic religion and quantum physics encourage me in that direction.

Question:

Your response was very interesting and certainly not without merit. However, in my post I stated that the one distinct aspect that a person has in order to set their beliefs in motion is "Faith". One must choose to accept science for what it is and what it says, yet at the same time make a conscious choice to believe or not that there is a God. I disagree that He is a "myth" as you put it. Jesus Christ was certainly not a myth and history can prove that. Whether he was the son of God or not might be debatable to some, though not for me.

True, God might not be able to be measured and tested in a scientific way, however for the person who looks for the evidence that He is real--they can find it.

Answer by Dr. Ashby

The idea I was getting at was that according to the Eastern philosophy, faith can be an initial motivator but that it does not serve well as a goal. In other words it is a means to an end and not an end in itself. The term "myth" is used differently in Western as opposed to Eastern culture. In Western culture myth means lie or primitive story to explain reality that is not true, based on ignorant notions, etc. In Eastern, African and Native American religious understanding, myth means vehicle to convey religious teachings and philosophies, but is not necessarily factual or historical or literal but contains transcendental truths. So the myth allows us to ask questions and embark on a journey of self-discovery. In science the hypothesis is the faith and the experiment is the journey and the discovery is the goal. We must also be clear that indeed whatever a person wants to be they will be in the end but that does not mean that what they have become is real. It may be real to them but not in objective fact. Discovering god through faith because a person wants to would be no different than finding a love affair which one was seeking or the right house one was seeking. The faith based discovery is within a worldly

The Limits of Faith

context and within the mental operations of the faithful and what they discover will be sustained by faith and not by universal reality. What I mean is that the house or the spouse that was found will someday bring pain, will someday be lost, etc. the true attainment of something is that which by definition cannot be lost. Whatever can be lost or can prove to be painful is not abidingly real but rather only real in a relative sense in time and space. If god can only be sustained through faith it is not the full God discovery that full religion is meant to find, but the limited notion of the faithful. The mystics discover the Divine in themselves and in Creation and that Divine is ever-present, meaning was there all along. They do not sustain it, it is self sustaining, and they have no need of faith since they realized their oneness with that existence which requires no effort, no self-delusion or constant proselytizing to convince others and sustain one's own faith.

The Theory of Evolution, the Conflict with Historical Religion and a Correct Path to Knowing

One of the most enduring questions of human existence is where we came from and its related question, how did we come to be? Throughout most of organized human existence human societies have sought to answer those questions through myths and religions. The corollary of that process led to cosmologies and metaphysical theories that related human existence to a god, goddess or gods and goddesses. However, when the joint 1858 paper by Charles Darwin and Alfred Russel Wallace was published, it proposed a different form of evolution than what was discussed in Western (Abrahamic) religious cosmogony theories that include a causal god. This difference has led to a controversy which continues to this day, between Creationism, the religious view of cosmogony and the Theory of Evolution, the scientific view of cosmogony. In this paper I will explore the questions of what the theory of evolution by natural selection is and what problems it may or may not resolve in reference to our understanding of where the world and human life came from {Cosmogony}. Also, I will look at what metaphysical implications there may be related to the evolutionary description of how transformation of species may take place.

In religious studies there is a term known as **"way of reasoned inquiry"**[i] defined as:

> **way of reasoned inquiry**: A rational, dialectical struggle to transcend conventional patterns of thinking in the effort attain understanding of, and consciousness-transforming insight into, what is taken to be the ultimate what, how, and why of things--i.e., to bring together and unite, so far as possible, mind with what is taken to be the ultimate Mind and thereby acquire a portion of divine wisdom. It typically

---

[i] **GENERAL RELIGIOUS STUDIES TERMS**
http://www.wou.edu/las/humanities/cannon/r201glos.htm

The Limits of Faith

involves systematic study of a tradition's scripture and previous attempts to articulate what is ultimately the case.

In religion the way of inquiry uses study of a religious scripture to gain insights into some ultimate essence of being. The Western religions, being historical[i] in nature necessarily seek to affirm a particular and definitive revelation of reality based on historical events in those religions. However, the Western religious theories[ii] about the existence of god ultimately involve a metaphysical force that cannot be definitively proven but the supposedly historical religious scriptures that are used to support the idea of its existence can be disproved by science.

The theory of evolution and origin of species referred to as "survival of the fittest" was called by Charles Darwin "Natural Selection" Darwin held that natural selection is a constant (daily, hourly) review of variations in living beings all around the world that works towards the "improvement of each organic being in relation to its …conditions of life". This means that a living being is constantly changing at a fundamental level (today known to be genetic) and that each change is evaluated to determine if the change is viable and beneficial to the survival of the particular organism in question; If it is found to be beneficial and a help to survival the change is maintained or selected and the being goes on and its offspring survive. The theory of evolution acknowledges millions of years of evolutionary time to produce significant changes over time and is contrasted with artificial selection or the deliberate process of selective breeding of living beings in order to produce particular changes or characteristics in their progeny. Examples of selective breeding or artificial selection include dog breeding or eugenics and human segregation.

---

[i] **historical religion**: A religious tradition which conceives itself to have originated in (or have been decisively shaped by) a revelation of "ultimate reality" intervening in human history through certain particular events, persons, and circumstances. Its central story will tell of a decisive revelation of trans-historical, universal significance as having actually taken place in historical time. In consequence, all efforts to convey the content of that alleged revelation will be shaped and colored by those historical particulars, and the tradition will continue to be preoccupied with those historical particulars as having been vested with eternal significance. The Western family of religions are all historical religions in this sense.

[ii] The Cosmological argument, ontological argument, pantheistic argument, inductive reasoning. teleological argument, Anthropic argument, Moral argument, transcendental argument, witness argument or personal experience arguments, etc.

The Limits of Faith

The Western religions generally reject the theory of evolution as it is based on a scientific **way of reasoned inquiry,** based on empirical evidences, that does not assume an ultimate essential divine being as the cause of existence which they term Creation and its corollary philosophy, "Creationism." For example, the Western religious theory of Creation acknowledges less than 10,000 thousand years to Cosmogony and history or the time from Creation to the present. The theory of evolution also holds that each evolutionary changes produces a new being because the as Darwin put it "Not one living species will transmit its unaltered likeness to a distant futurity." In a "historical religion" the ideal is that the same beings who received the ultimate revolutionary history are the same as the descendants. Therefore, the evolutionary theory via natural selection would be in direct contradiction to the religious dogma even if the religious group attempted to segregate itself from other populations since natural selection occurs even within specific populations as well as the entire population of a species because of environmental differences and other natural organic processes within the body. So the people who existed when the Western religions were created were not physically (genetically) the same as the people who descended from their genetic material who are living today. Therefore, if there was a supposed physical reality that was ultimate for those people who existed in the past and was designed for them how could that same ultimate physical and historical reality work for people today who are physically different and living in a different time?

Such conundrums as the problem caused by the historicity claim of the Western religions have led to contradictions and conflict between those religions with each other and with other non-Western religions over which religion is "true" or "real" and therefore correct, since correctness would be based on the veracity of a religion which would itself be based on its supposed historicity. Thus, if a religion cannot claim historical and absolute revelation it cannot be real or true and would therefore be considered heathenish and therefore also blasphemous and consequently worthy of eradication so that the "true" religion may exist alone and without erroneous detractors trying to tear it (true religion) down or contaminate it.

Critics of the theory of evolution might say that the Theory of evolution does not answer all the scientific questions because not enough scientific evidence from the fossil record has been recovered. However, what has been collected sufficiently proves the framework of the theory which is why the vast majority of scientists adhere to it. So in that sense the theory of evolution creates problems in that it cannot be definitively proven and so opens the door to religious detractors. In a wider sense it leads to or exacerbates conflict in society between religionists and those who believe in science or who are atheists or agnostics where there was no conflict before or where the conflict was only between believers in the religious cosmogony or none at all, prior to the introduction of the theory of evolution which provides new arguments for those who do not believe in religion to counter or detract from it.

The *orthodoxy* (*emphasizing correct beliefs*) in Western religions would seem to outweigh their *orthopraxis* (emphasizing correct (ethical) behavior) since they hold that there is or was a metaphysical causal impetus that created the universe and human beings as they are today and that one should act in accordance with that belief and exclude other beliefs. For the fundamentalist religious believer, the fundamental belief that God created the world takes precedence over the belief that God created all life and all human beings, even those with different beliefs. Therefore, the commandment not to kill or to love the neighbor as oneself would be secondary in the fundamentalist belief system, thereby allowing such a personality to commit acts that break the "lower" injunctions in support of the primary or fundamental ones. Further, the theory of evolution would uphold the understanding that all human beings had a common ancestor and therefore a common history and presumably a common fate (eschatology). This would mean that the concept in some religions that there is a special "chosen" group above others, that would have a different fate, based on their history or heredity, would be impossible.

Metaphysics, as an adjunct theory within cosmogony, that God or some divinity created the universe and all life as they now are, would tend to be upset by the contention within the theory of evolution that present species developed to their current state out of primitive forms instead of being ready made and placed on earth by a god figure. We should distinguish between Western and Eastern /African metaphysics. The Eastern and African would say that the creation, through whatever process, proceeds from the mind of God, while the Western claims it occurred historically at a particular point in history, the beginning, which was just a few thousand years ago, which is actually after the founding of Ancient Egyptian civilization. Thus, Ancient Egypt did not apparently exist when archeologists and geologists proved it did (10,000-7,000 B.C.E.) but rather 4,000 when the Bible scholars say the world began. So the orthodox conceptions being governed by the rule of orthodoxy must necessarily contradict and reject all contrary theories be they based on scientific evidences or not. Therefore, to the historical religion it is more important to have and uphold certain "correct beliefs" than to have "proven beliefs" or beliefs based on empirical, physical or tangible evidences. In other words, it is more important for the orthodox religion to have dogmas than to have proven truths since the dogmas are believed to be the ultimate realities.

It is interesting to note that the theory of Evolution, while it has had a great impact on Western culture and other cultures around the world, has not had the effect of debunking religion even though it would apparently disprove the historicity of historical religions. For example, scientific evidences support beyond reasonable doubt that a worldwide flood never occurred and that the cosmogony of Genesis in the Bible of the Western religions did not occur; yet there still are believers and more adherents join them as world strife increases. Therefore, ontological arguments for the existence of God that are based on metaphysical arguments and supported by historical dogmas would seem to be baseless. It is also notable those scientific revolutions could occur at all in the presence of orthodox religion and that some of the scientists are also believers in orthodox religions as if the two ideas can coexist in harmony; it would seem that they are present in the same personality but are not reconciled. In such a personality the religious theory seems to exist independent of intellectual inquiry {critical thinking} while the scientific theories are also devoid of ontological inquiry, being relegated only to practical applications for survival and social profit through the use of scientific discoveries to conduct commerce or create advancements for conveniences or war implements to secure resources.

This way of being would seem to be devoid of peace and wisdom; peace through resolution of the internal conflict (ignorance through lack of progress in religious inquiry due to following limited religion) which leads to external conflicts and wars and wisdom to discover how both metaphysics and physics can be harmonized in order to lead to a true discovery of what epistemology will lead to a correct ontology about the cosmos. A comedian once pointed out that Christian oil company executives want to have it both ways, they want to "live in the Garden of Eden while working in Jurassic Park," he explained: "its an impossible commute" since they want to believe in the Bible which says human beings came into existence only a few years ago by the hand of God, but the science of fossil fuels relates to the understanding of evolution through millions of years. The recognition of this contradiction and the seeming irrational denial of evolution by some followers of religion which is perceived as hypocrisy or willful ignorance by many observers may be a strong contributing factor which impels many people away from organized Western religions and to consider themselves as "spiritual but not religious." In this context the term "religious" is increasingly becoming equated with orthodoxy, irrationality, dogmatism, exclusivist and condemnation of anything that is different from the dogma.

When people speak of being "spiritual" they are really seeking true meaning beyond dogmas and that can be discovered when a correct path to knowing is practiced. In such practice religious historicity takes a back seat to religious experience. In such practice people necessarily must leave behind primitive notions of faith-based religious practice which reaches only the level of myth and ritual (religion has three stages: *Myth, Ritual and Mysticism*). From a theological perspective this is what people who want to promote harmony among the religions must work towards – if possible. However, the greatest benefit will be for themselves, since the masses are hard to change especially when led by demagogs. Nevertheless, they should work to change their own personal perspective and that in itself will change their associations and congregations in some small degree.

The Limits of Faith

More Q & A

Question:

Your discourse about religion and the way of looking at life, Eastern versus Western, has opened up some issues that maybe you can clear up. Can you tell me if it is Vedic thought that the universe is continually collapsing and expanding, similar to the oscillating theory?

Answer by Dr. Ashby:

Greetings, and thank you for your kind words and thank you for engaging in such a delicate subject with such openness and lucidity.

The Vedic {Hindu Mysticism} as well as the Neterian {Ancient Egyptian Mysticism} both do not specifically see a collapsing and expanding universe in the same way as the Western model does. However, perhaps the word oscillating is more appropriate. The understanding in the Vedic tradition is that of cycles or periods called Yuga in which the universe goes from created to uncreated and then the cycle repeats. In Vedanta-Hindu myth the end of all yugas is followed by Pralaya or the dissolution. God {Krishna-Vishnu} dissolves Creation.

In the Neterian cycle, Creation is created when the God Ra emerges on his boat to sail the primeval ocean. The wake produced by his boat creates waves or vibrations that ripple through the entire ocean, polarizing matter and causing it to take form. When he tires after "Millions and millions" of years he retires back to the ocean and the world dissolves back into its original essence. Then after an indeterminate time (time does not exist during the dissolution) he emerges again to start the Creation all over.

The Limits of Faith

Question:

This question is about technology and proving the existence of God through technology or relying on faith. While we have a source (atoms and electrons-which may not be seen individually but can be seen and felt physically) from which to observe the effects on mater, we do not have a God to see or feel physically to determine of that God is having direct effects on Matter. I am not sure this ties into identifying God so much, but I am astounded at the idea that our outside intention can affect behavior of quantum particles. How **does** that work into a God definition?.

Answer by Dr. Ashby:

In Chapter 1 of his book, *Red Giants and White Dwarfs,* Mr. Jastrow discussed the existence of the electron. Being so small it could not be seen but yet its existence was theorized or assumed based on its effects or rather the interactions observed in certain kinds of matter. The situation with the "discovery" of the electron could be likened to the belief in the existence of God if we assume that Creation was Created by someone or something. However, the situation is different because while we have a source (atoms and electrons-which may not be seen individually but can be seen and felt physically) from which to observe the effects on matter, we do not have a God to see or feel physically to determine of that *God is having direct effects on Matter*. Again, if we assume that god created things and set them in motion in the beginning we could ascribe that effect to god but that would be un-provable and therefore, again, merely an assumption.

Such exercises, experiments on matter or theoretical constructs, such as those of Stephen Hawking, would seem to lead us in circles, probably because what we are examining (Creation) and the instrument we are using to examine (mind) are inadequate for the task. Yet the Eastern, African and Native American indigenous religious traditions, have claimed, from ancient times, that the means to discover truth is not with the physical senses or the mind but through intuition, developed through training of the higher sense that can allow a human being to transcend time and space itself to a level of communion with nature directly, without the need for cumbersome mental concepts, theories or faith.

The Limits of Faith

Quantum physics is a fascinating area that with every new year seems to look more and more like an eastern mystic set of theories. In the book The Tao of Physics, the author Fritjof Capra sought to show that the mystic concepts of life are not incompatible with the new discoveries of modern physics. For instance, the mystic understanding of matter has been that the primeval ocean is a metaphor signifying an indeterminate preexisting substance [that goes to make up formed matter], or undifferentiated matter (matter without form). The Eastern and African Creation myth speaks of the divine egg and the emergence of God (consciousness) from the primeval ocean. Modern physics now tells us that matter originally came from one point out of which all matter emerged. Even right now it rises from an indeterminate source into time and space and then passes back into "nothingness" and going "nowhere". Now modern physics speaks of dark matter or quantum realms that transcend our physical reality.

The mystic understanding has been, for thousands of years, that the universe is actually a projection of the consciousness of God and not an actual and physical reality. Here comes modern physics now to tell us that matter is not actually solid but a projection of quantum events or strings, etc. In this respect the mystic philosophy would not need to adjust anything and a mystic would have no difficulty reading the Bhagavad Gita text of India or the PertmHeru text of Ancient Egypt and then read the theories of Stephen Hawking. The mystic does not look to matter but to the force behind it that directs it and from which it arose.

While it is fascinating to consider the quantum theories as well as the mystic ones it is important to realize that our investigation instruments, the mind and senses are extremely limited. This is why the sages have admonished mystic students to go beyond the mind and senses in order to experience the transcendental reality directly, without the distorting intermediary mediums.

Some Yogis and Eastern mystics have likened the mystic eastern concepts to the Western Christian and Jewish and Islamic mystic teachings of the Gnostics, Kabbalists and Sufis respectively. These western mystic traditions try to go beyond the orthodox teachings to "experience" oneness with God which might be termed as "Kingdom of Heaven" in the sense that Jesus said the kingdom was within us – and not outside. Modern physics also theorizes that every point in the universe is central to it. In this way we can correlate the mystic teaching that not only God is everywhere and that God is manifesting everything and that the innermost reality of everything is God or Consciousness and no part is more important than another since all is essentially one; So God is One, we are one; we (Creation, people, animals, planets, etc.) are God.

Therefore, since we are God we are architects of Creation and our lives, or we may say our individual souls co-create with God as a drop co-creates wetness with the ocean. So we are those quantum particles and we move them in accordance with and to the extent of our understanding of what and who we are.

The Limits of Faith
NOTES

1 The Perennial Philosophy (Latin philosophia perennis) is the idea that a universal set of truths common to all people and cultures exists. The term was first used by the German mathematician and philosopher Gottfried Leibniz to designate the common, eternal philosophy that underlies all religious movements, in particular the mystical streams within them. The term was later popularized by Aldous Huxley in his 1945 book The Perennial Philosophy. The term "perennial philosophy" has also been used to translate the concept of the "eternal or perennial truth" in the Sanskrit Sanatana Dharma.

The concept of perennial philosophy is the fundamental tenet of the Traditionalist School, formalized in the writings of 20th century metaphysicians René Guénon and Frithjof Schuon. The Indian scholar and writer Ananda Coomaraswamy, associated with the Traditionalists, also wrote extensively about the perennial philosophy.

http://en.wikipedia.org/wiki/Perennial_philosophy

2 African Origins of Civilization, by Muata Ashby, Mystical Journey From Jesus to Christ, by Muata Ashby

3 Essential Judiasm: A Complete Guide to Beliefs, Customs and Rituals by George Robinson (Pocket Books, 2000). "Torah, Torah, Torah: The Unfolding of a Tradition." Judaism for Dummies (Hungry Minds, 2001). Tracey R. Rich, "Torah." Judaism 101 (1995-99).

4 While the term Jewish is used largely as a religious or and ethnic designation it is actually a religious designation or name.

5 Jewish Life in Ancient Egypt by Edward Bleiberg for the Brooklyn Museum 2002

6 Zealot A member of a Jewish movement of the first century A.D. that fought against Roman rule in Palestine as incompatible with strict monotheism. Source: The American Heritage® Dictionary of the English Language, Fourth Edition Copyright © 2000 by Houghton Mifflin Company

7 1. George Robinson, Essential Judaism (Pocket Books, 2000), 541-50. 2. John Bowker, ed., Cambridge Illustrated History of Religions. 3. "Judaism." Encyclopædia Britannica (Encyclopædia Britannica Premium Service, 2004).

8 Jewish Life in Ancient Egypt by Edward Bleiberg. Egyptian Mysteries Vol. 2: The Gods and Goddesses of the Ancient Egyptians by Muata Ashby

9 Mystical journey From Jesus to Christ by Muata Ashby, 1998, p. 55

10 Random House Encyclopedia Copyright (C) 1983,1990 by Random House Inc.

11 Essential Judiasm: A Complete Guide to Beliefs, Customs and Rituals by George Robinson (Pocket Books, 2000). "Torah, Torah, Torah: The Unfolding of a Tradition." Judaism for Dummies (Hungry Minds, 2001). Tracey R. Rich, "Torah." Judaism 101 (1995-99).

12 "Talmud and Midrash." Encyclopædia Britannica. Encyclopædia Britannica Premium Service (2004). Essential Judiasm: A Complete Guide to Beliefs, Customs and Rituals by George Robinson (Pocket Books, 2000). "Torah, Torah, Torah: The Unfolding of a Tradition." Judaism for Dummies (Hungry Minds, 2001). Tracey R. Rich, "Torah." Judaism 101 (1995-99).

13 Contemporary Zoroastrians: An Unstructured Nation. Lanham, MD: University Press of America. Zaehner, R.C. 1961. (Zaehner, 20-21)

14 Zoroastrianism: an Ethnic Perspective. Bombay: Good Impressions. (Ramazani, 21) Ramazani, Nesta. 1997.

15 [http://news.bbc.co.uk/2/hi/americas/4317498.stm, White House denies Bush God claim The White House has dismissed as "absurd" allegations made in a BBC TV series that President Bush claimed God told him to invade Iraq.]

16 According to Palestinian negotiator Nabil Shaath, said by Bush to him, apparently in the same June 2003 meeting, as reported by BBC News. Shaath later disclaimed the quote. [http://news.bbc.co.uk/2/hi/americas/4320586.stm, Bush God comments 'not literal' A Palestinian official who said the US president had claimed God told him to invade Iraq and Afghanistan says he did not take George Bush's words literally.], Denied by White House spokesperson Scott McClellan, October 6, 2005, and by Mahmoud Abbas who attended the meeting in question. [http://www.smh.com.au/news/world/abbas-denies-bushs-mission-from-god-remark/2005/10/08/1128563027485.html, Abbas denies Bush's 'mission from God' remark, October 8, 2005 - 12:23PM

The Limits of Faith

17 Without a Doubt By Ron Suskind The New York Times, Saturday 17 October 2004 [Ron Suskind was the senior national-affairs reporter for The Wall Street Journal from 1993 to 2000. He is the author most recently of "The Price of Loyalty: George W. Bush, the White House and the Education of Paul O'Neill."]

18 Democracy Now.org Fmr. GOP Strategist Kevin Phillips on American Theocracy: The Peril and Politics of Radical Religion, Oil, and Borrowed Money in the 21st Century 3-21-06

19 According to the Biblical account.

20 From Wikipedia Encyclopedia, http://en.wikipedia.org/wiki/Abraham

21 concept of the creation of a Jewish homeland-promised land

22 see the full history in the book Mystical Journey From Jesus to Christ by Muata Ashby

23 A dean at Harvard University and a professor at the University of Chicago are coming under intense criticism for publishing an academic critique of the pro-Israel lobby in Washington. The paper charges that the United States has willingly set aside its own security and that of many of its allies, in order to advance the interests of Israel. In addition, the study accuses the pro-Israel lobby, particularly AIPAC, the America Israel Public Affairs Committee, of manipulating the U.S. media, policing academia and silencing critics of Israel by labeling them as anti-Semitic. The study also examines the role played by the pro-Israel neoconservatives in the lead-up to the U.S. invasion of Iraq. Democracy Now.org Friday, March 31st, 2006 EXCLUSIVE...Noam Chomsky on Failed States: The Abuse of Power and the Assault on Democracy

24 From Wikipedia encyclopedia

25 Democracy Now.org Fmr. GOP Strategist Kevin Phillips on American Theocracy: The Peril and Politics of Radical Religion, Oil, and Borrowed Money in the 21st Century 3-21-06

26 Quoted from the book : Tim LaHaye (September 1998). Rapture: Under Attack, Multnomah Publishers.

27 From Wikipedia encyclopedia

28 ibid

29 The Columbia Electronic Encyclopedia Copyright © 2004, Columbia University Press.

30 The Mystical Journey from Jesus to Christ by Muata Ashby

31 Anderson's Constitutions (1723) the bylaws of the Grand Lodge of England,

32 The Columbia Electronic Encyclopedia Copyright © 2004, Columbia University Press.

33 A member of a group of English Protestants who in the 16th and 17th centuries advocated strict religious discipline along with simplification of the ceremonies and creeds of the Church of England. Source: The American Heritage® Dictionary of the English Language, Fourth Edition Copyright © 2000

34 who in the year 2005 publicly advocated the assassination of Hugo Chavez, the president of Venezuela

35 From Wikipedia encyclopedia

36 http://www.pfaw.org/pfaw/general/default.aspx?oid=4307 People for the American Way

 Founded in: 1989 Membership: Claims nearly 2 million members, but other data suggests 300,000-400,000 members.

37 http://en.wikipedia.org/wiki/Theocracy

38 http://www.washingtonpost.com/wp-dyn/content/article/2006/03/21/AR2006032101723.html

39 PBS NOW, with David Brincoccio

40 http://www.sullivan-county.com/news/pat_quotes/big_lie.htm, Date (2/22/00)

41 http://mediamatters.org/items/200508220006

42 http://www.latimes.com/news/local/la-me-allsaints7nov07,0,6769876.story?coll=la-home-headlines, LATimes archive.

43 http://www.dfw.com/mld/dfw/living/religion/14176450.htm, By Jim Jones

Special to the Star-Telegram, Posted on Sat, Mar. 25, 2006

email this

print this

The Limits of Faith

44 http://mediamatters.org/items/200603160009, Thu, Mar 16, 2006 5:00pm EST, In an ABC Nightline segment featuring Rev. Franklin Graham's controversial comments about Islam

45 March 13 broadcast of CBN's The 700 Club, http://mediamatters.org/items/200603140008

46 African Origins of Civilization by Muata Ashby

47 present day Palestine

48 African Origins of Western Civilization, Religion and Philosophy- by Dr. Muata Ashby,

49 One example among many is Jerusalem Countdown: A Warning to the World by Pastor John Hagee

50 "Exodus," Microsoft (R) Encarta. Copyright (c) 1994 Microsoft Corporation. Copyright (c) 1994 Funk & Wagnall's Corporation.

51 See Mystical Journey From Jesus to Christ

52 MICHAEL G. HASEL Department of Near Eastern Studies

53 Merriam-Webster Online Dictionary

54 Mahabharata (Sanskrit, Great Story), longer of the two great epic poems of ancient India; the other is the Ramayana. The Mahabharata was composed beginning about 300B.C.E. and received numerous additions until about 300 A.C.E.. "Mahabharata," Microsoft® Encarta® Encyclopedia 2000. © 1993-1999 Microsoft Corporation. All rights reserved.

55 Any of a group of philosophical treatises contributing to the theology of ancient Hinduism-Vedanta Philosophy, elaborating on and superseding the earlier Vedas.

56 "Cambyses II," Microsoft (R) Encarta. Copyright (c) 1994 Microsoft Corporation. Copyright (c) 1994 Funk & Wagnall's Corporation.

57 The Black Ancient Egyptians by Muata Ashby, Egypt Child of Africa by Ivan Van Sertima

58 a criminal offence that supposedly goes beyond simple lobbying and political contributions

59 Mr. Kennedy serves as Chief Prosecuting Attorney for the Hudson Riverkeeper and President of Waterkeeper Alliance. He is also a Clinical Professor and Supervising Attorney at Pace University School of Law's Environmental Litigation Clinic and is co-host of Ring of Fire on Air America Radio. Earlier in his career he served as Assistant District Attorney in New York City. He has worked on several political campaigns including the presidential campaigns of Edward M. Kennedy in 1980, Al Gore in 2000 and John Kerry in 2004. http://www.robertfkennedyjr.com/about.html

60 author of Divine Destruction: Dominion Theology and American Environmental Policy (Melville Manifestos) Stephenie Hendricks

61 Ring of Fire- Air America Radio interview Stephenie Hendricks March 4, 2006

62 http://www.cbsnews.com/stories/2006/04/12/eveningnews/main1494758.shtml

63 http://web.amnesty.org/library/index/engafr540762004

64 From Wikipedia Encyclopedia

65 ibid

66 ibid

67 "The Isis Papers" by Dr. Frances Cress-Welsing

68 United Nations World Conference on Racism, Durban So. Africa.

69 See the books The Mystical Journey From Jesus to Christ by Muata Ashby, Nag Hammadi Library, edited by James Robinson "The Other Bible" translated by Wilhelm Schneemelcher, New Testament Apocrypha

70 United Nations World Conference on Racism, Durban So. Africa.

71 Meditations on First Philosophy by Rene Descartes Translated by John Veitch (1901)

72 Wikipedia encyclopedia

73 ibid

The Limits of Faith

INDEX

Abermoff, Jack -US Congress bribery scandal, 69
Abraham, 27, 46, 51, 53, 87, 88, 92, 96, 100, 162
Absolute, 128, 145
Acts, 94
Adams, John, 34
Afghanistan, 25, 87, 161
Afghanistan War, 87
Africa, 3, 60, 72, 75, 76, 85, 91, 94, 101, 111, 128, 129, 163
African American, 36, 56, 57, 66
African Religion, 120
African religions, 12
Agnostic, 137, 148
Ahura Mazda, 14
Air, 37, 163
Air America Radio, 37, 163
Air, Clean air, 37, 163
Albert Einstein, 125
Albright, Madeline, 23, 24
Alexander the Great, 54, 86
Alexandria, 54, 86
Allah, 18, 86, 93, 98, 99, 100, 101, 102
Amen, 56
American Heritage Dictionary, Dictionary, 5, 161, 162, 163
American Theocracy, 162
American way of life, 42
Americas, 35, 59, 65, 76, 91
Ancient Egypt, 3, 7, 8, 9, 10, 11, 12, 15, 22, 31, 33, 40, 46, 48, 51, 52, 53, 54, 56, 57, 63, 84, 86, 98, 101, 105, 110, 111, 129, 139, 140, 144, 145, 148, 155, 157, 159, 161, 163
Ancient Greeks, 104
Angra Mainyu, 13, 14
Apocalyptic, 14
Apocalypticism, 28, 29
Apocrypha, 163
Aquarian Gospel, 41, 60, 79
Arabia, 41, 60, 79

Arab-Muslim, 60, 77, 78, 101
Arabs, 27, 28, 43, 75, 76, 77, 80, 92, 98, 100, 106
Ari, 64
Aristotle, 127
Armageddon, 26, 42, 43, 147
Aryan, 15, 52
Aryans, 52
Asar, 8, 86, 101, 144
Aset, 8
Aset (Isis), 8
Asia, 51, 53, 56, 60, 72, 74, 76, 98
Asia XE "Asia" Minor, 51, 56, 60
Asia Minor, 74
Asia Minor, 76
Asia Minor, 98
Asia Minor, 98
Asians, 100
Assurance Age, 4, 7, 9, 10, 14
Assyrian, 55
Assyrians, 7
Atman, 108
Atum, 144, 145
Awakening, 79
Babylon, 32
Babylonians, 21
Balfour Declaration of 1917, 27
BBC, 161
Being, 8, 10, 11, 14, 15, 33, 34, 72, 126, 141, 144, 158
Berber, 76, 77
Bhagavad Gita, 110, 159
Bible, 5, 10, 12, 19, 27, 28, 29, 33, 43, 45, 46, 47, 51, 52, 53, 54, 57, 61, 63, 82, 83, 86, 87, 88, 89, 90, 92, 94, 95, 97, 99, 100, 120, 130, 134, 135, 137, 141, 146, 148, 155, 156, 163
Big Bang, 129
Black, 76, 107
Book of Revelation, Christian bible, new testament, 14

164

Book of the Dead, see also Rau Nu Prt M Hru, 110
Brahman, 53, 108, 145
British empire, 61
Brooklyn Museum, 161
bubble, real estate, 121
Buber, Martin, 106
Buddha, 8, 40, 105, 115, 116, 120, 137, 148
Buddha Consciousness, 137
Buddhism, 3, 8, 41, 55, 127, 130, 134, 137
Buddhist, 86, 106, 130, 137, 148
Bush administration, 24, 36, 38
Bush, George W., 23, 24, 36, 39, 69, 79, 162
Byzantine, 75, 86
Campbell, Joseph, 84, 143
Canaan, 43, 48, 51, 60, 89, 90
Canada, 36
career counselor, career, job, 163
Career, Job, 95, 148
Catholic, 12, 19, 31, 55, 61, 65, 96, 146
Catholic Church, 31, 55, 61, 65, 96
Catholic XE "Roman Catholic" s, 35, 63, 95
Chandogya Upanishad, 145
Charismatic, 29
Charismatic XE "Charismatic" Churches, 29
Charlemagne, 60, 65
Chaves, Hugo, 71, 162
Child, 163
China, 79, 128
Chomsky, Noam, 162
Christ, 9, 15, 40, 41, 42, 53, 56, 61, 62, 63, 74, 97, 101, 102, 119, 137, 161, 162, 163
Christ Consciousness, 15, 97, 137
Christhood, 120
Christian Church, 17
Christian Colleges, 4, 68
Christianity, 4, 5, 9, 10, 11, 12, 14, 15, 17, 18, 20, 21, 29, 30, 31, 33, 35, 40, 42, 43, 47, 55, 56, 58, 63, 64, 65, 77, 79, 83, 86, 87, 90, 92, 95, 96, 97, 98, 120, 131, 144
Christians, eastern, 78
Church, 17, 31, 38, 39, 55, 61, 65, 75, 96, 137, 162
Church of England, 162
Circuit, 69
Civilization, 161, 163
Class, ruling class, 34, 65, 72
Coffin Texts, 144, 145
colonialism, 72, 80, 98
Conflict, 4, 86, 151
Confucianism, 3, 8
Confucius, 8
Congress, 2, 33, 69
Consciousness, 16, 97, 137, 143, 160
Consciousness, human, 130
Constantine, 60
Constitution, 123
Corinthians, 94
cosmic force, 139
Cosmogony, 151, 153
Council for National Policy, 30
Counter-Reversion Era, 4, 7, 8, 9, 10
Creation, 8, 11, 14, 72, 105, 115, 123, 129, 136, 139, 142, 143, 144, 145, 150, 153, 157, 158, 159, 160
Creationism, 4, 129, 131, 136, 151, 153
Cross, 9
Crusades, 19, 60, 65, 74, 75
Culture, 103
Cyrus the Great, Persian emperor, 13
Danger, 4, 45
Darwin, 151, 152, 153
Darwin, Charles, 151, 152, 153
Davos, Party of, 34
Death, 62
Democracy Now, 162
Democratic Party, 29, 30, 36, 44
Descartes, 22, 23, 109, 110, 112, 122, 163
Devil, 80, 113
Dharma, 161
Diebold Inc, 37
Dionysius, 86
Dionysius the Areopagite, 86

Dionysius the Areopagite, 86
Dionysus the Areopagite, 86
Discipline, 3
Disraeli, Benjamin, 26, 27
divine incarnation, 52
DNA, 59
Dominionism, 28, 29
drug companies, 125
Earth, 96
economic subjugation, 81
Egyptian Mysteries, 15, 161
Egyptian religion, 7, 8, 9, 12, 33, 56, 63, 98, 101, 129
Egyptian Yoga see also Kamitan Yoga, 3
Elohim, 11
end times, 28, 42, 43
Enlightenment, 104, 120
Essenes, 10
Ethics, 57
Ethiopia, 94
Ethnic, 161
Eucharist, 9
Europe, 26, 32, 34, 35, 43, 60, 74, 75, 76, 78, 80, 84, 87, 90, 94, 101
Evangelical, 29, 63, 79
Evangelicals, 35, 116
Evolution, theory of, 4, 129, 131, 151, 155
Existence, 145
Eye, 87
eye for an eye, 19
Failed States, 162
Fairness Doctrine, 35
Faith, 2, 4, 5, 6, 102, 103, 122, 129, 131, 149
faith-based, 9, 15, 16, 17, 18, 19, 20, 21, 22, 23, 24, 25, 26, 37, 72, 83, 103, 134, 135, 156
Falashas, 94
FCC, 35
Federalist Society, 69
financial collapse, 71
Fire, 163
flexible currency, 34
Food, 124

Founding Fathers, 123
France, 33, 75
Freemasonry, 32, 33
Freemasons, 32, 33, 34
Fundamentalism, 72
fundamentalists, 26, 29, 33, 35, 38, 43, 72, 112, 116
Fundamentalists, 19
Garden of Eden, 156
Gaul, 60, 74
Genes, 59
Genghis Khan, 98
Germany, 31, 66
Ghandi, Mahatma, 18
Gnostic, 12, 15, 31, 32, 95, 120, 137, 149
Gnostic Christianity, 12
Gnostic XE "Gnostic" Gospels, 95
Gnostic Gospels, 137
Gnostics, 12, 159
God, 5, 8, 11, 12, 13, 14, 15, 16, 17, 18, 20, 22, 23, 24, 25, 27, 29, 31, 37, 40, 41, 42, 45, 46, 48, 51, 52, 53, 55, 56, 61, 62, 72, 79, 86, 87, 88, 89, 90, 91, 92, 94, 97, 99, 101, 102, 109, 111, 112, 116, 119, 123, 126, 131, 132, 133, 136, 137, 138, 139, 141, 142, 143, 144, 145, 146, 147, 148, 149, 150, 154, 155, 156, 157, 158, 159, 160, 161
God XE "God" Framework, 11
Goddess, 8
Goddesses, 161
Gods, 8, 52, 161
gods and goddesses, 7, 11, 14, 139, 144, 151
Good, 79, 161
Gore, Al, 36, 163
Gospels, 11, 95, 137
Graham, Franklin, 40, 41, 163
Great Awakening, 79
Great Pyramid, 53
Great Pyramids, 53
Greece, 8
Greek philosophers, 104, 113
Greek Philosophy, 103
Greeks, 56, 83, 104

The Limits of Faith

Gulf War, 87
Haiti, 65
Ham, 61
Health, 3
Hearing, 100
Heart, 137
Heart (also see Ab, mind, conscience), 137
Heaven, 95, 96, 132, 133, 137, 159
Hebrew, 10, 11, 12, 27, 45, 46, 51, 54, 57, 88, 90
Hebrew Bible, 10
Hebrews, 10, 27, 51, 86
Hegemony, 4, 45
Henotheism, 4, 7
Hermeticism, 86
Herodotus, 54, 94
Heru, 10, 101
Heru (see Horus), 10, 101
Hindu, 102, 148, 157
Hindu religion, 102
Hinduism, 18, 41, 52, 134, 163
Hitler, 61
Hittites, 89, 92
Holy Land, 27, 75, 78
Holy Spirit, 31, 79
Horus, 10
Hyksos, 47
Illuminati, 30, 31, 32, 34
imperialism, 71, 80, 131
India, 3, 7, 15, 52, 76, 84, 86, 110, 111, 121, 128, 144, 145, 159, 163
Indian Yoga, 3
Indra, 52
Intelligent Design, 131
Internal Revenue Service, 39
Iran, 81
Iraq, 24, 25, 36, 61, 65, 87, 161, 162
Isis, 8, 148, 163
Isis, See also Aset, 8, 148, 163
Islam, 4, 10, 18, 26, 40, 41, 42, 55, 58, 64, 65, 72, 74, 76, 77, 79, 80, 83, 86, 98, 99, 100, 101, 102, 163
Ismail (Ishmael), 100
Israel, 4, 26, 27, 43, 46, 47, 48, 51, 61, 63, 78, 80, 88, 89, 91, 92, 101, 162

Jacob (and Israel), 46, 88, 96, 100
Jainism, 8
Jefferson, Thomas, 32, 123
Jehova, 11
Jerusalem, 9, 13, 51, 75, 88, 163
Jesus, 10, 14, 15, 16, 17, 28, 40, 41, 42, 47, 53, 56, 61, 62, 63, 64, 75, 87, 91, 95, 97, 99, 100, 115, 116, 119, 120, 130, 137, 141, 148, 149, 159, 161, 162, 163
Jesus Christ, 40, 41, 61, 97, 149
Jewish, 4, 8, 10, 11, 12, 13, 14, 17, 22, 26, 27, 28, 45, 46, 47, 48, 51, 52, 53, 54, 56, 57, 58, 61, 63, 86, 87, 88, 90, 91, 92, 94, 95, 100, 101, 102, 103, 106, 119, 144, 159, 161, 162
Jewish Bible, 12, 27, 47, 54, 61
Jewish Mysticism, 106
Jewish XE "Jewish" people, 10, 27, 48, 53, 88, 90, 91
Jewish religion, 9, 10, 11, 51, 57, 63
Jewish state, 26, 27, 28, 61, 101
Jewish-Christian bible, 26
Jews, 9, 11, 12, 13, 18, 19, 22, 26, 27, 30, 42, 45, 46, 51, 52, 53, 54, 55, 56, 57, 58, 60, 61, 62, 63, 64, 66, 82, 87, 88, 90, 91, 92, 93, 94, 95, 96, 98, 99, 100, 101, 102
Jews, Egyptian, 9
Jews, Orthodox, 12, 30
Job, 95, 148
Joseph, 46, 53, 84, 143
Joseph Campbell, 84, 143
Judaism, 4, 8, 9, 10, 11, 12, 13, 15, 18, 21, 30, 35, 47, 54, 55, 56, 57, 58, 63, 64, 83, 86, 87, 92, 93, 94, 96, 98, 106, 144, 161
Judeo-Christian, 21, 22, 28, 41, 42, 43, 45, 47, 92, 98, 117, 148
Kamitan, 56, 102
Kennedy, John F. president, 69, 163
Kerry, John, 163
Khnum, 11
Kingdom, 57, 76, 95, 96, 97, 137, 139, 141, 159
Kingdom of heaven, 96

Kingdom of Heaven, 95, 96, 137, 139, 141, 159
Know Thyself, 124
Knowledge, 5
Koran, 18, 88, 92, 96, 98, 99, 100, 101, 102
Krishna, 40, 52, 120, 133, 148, 157
Kundalini, 3
Kundalini XE "Kundalini" Yoga see also Serpent Power, 3
Latin, 31, 161
left behind series, 30, 69
Life, 126, 161
Logos, 103, 104, 105
Love, 88, 104, 105, 113
Maat, 40
Mahabharata, 52, 163
Mahavira, 8
Marxism, 41
Masters, 3
Matter, 158
Matthew, 53, 61, 62, 87, 95, 96, 141
Maya, 111
medical system, 125
Medu Neter, 51
Memphite Theology, 139
Mesopotamia, 46
Metaphysics, 154
middle ages, 103
Middle Ages, 32, 74
Middle East, 7, 9, 10, 25, 27, 28, 43, 61, 72, 74, 78, 79, 80, 88, 92, 94
Middle East XE "Middle East" ern oil, 27
Mind, 151
Missionaries, 100
Modern physics, 159, 160
Moorish, 76
Moors, 76, 77
Moral Majority, 30
Morales, Evo, 71
Moses, 12, 45, 46, 47, 62, 88, 89, 100, 115, 116, 130
Muhammad, 40, 60, 80, 99, 101, 130
Mundaka Upanishad, 52
Music, 3
Muslims, 19, 27, 28, 41, 55, 60, 72, 74, 75, 77, 80, 86, 88, 91, 93, 98, 99, 100, 101
Mysteries, 15, 161
mystical philosophy, 8, 10, 54, 141
Mysticism, 3, 106, 147, 156, 157
NAFTA, 36
Nag Hammadi, 163
Native American, 61, 77, 100, 108, 111, 120, 129, 132, 149, 158
Native American XE "Native American" s, 61, 77, 100, 111, 120, 132
Native American XE "Native American" s See also American Indians, 61, 77, 100, 111, 120, 132
Nazi, 66
neo-con, 28, 34, 68, 79
neo-conservative, 28, 34, 79
neo-conservatives, 28, 34
Neter, 15, 51
Neterian, 157
Netherworld, 140
New Testament, 12, 14, 19, 29, 87, 95, 163
Nirvana, 137
Noah, 63
Nu, 145
Nubia, 3
Nubians, 57
nuclear weapons, 61, 80, 88, 131
Nun, 145
Nun (primeval waters-unformed matter), 145
Nun (See also Nu primeval waters-unformed matter), 111, 145
Nun (See also Nu), 145
Ohio, 36, 37
Old Testament, 12, 18, 19, 27, 29, 45, 47, 52, 54, 87, 90, 92
Orthodox, 11, 12, 21, 22, 30, 40, 65, 79, 83, 87, 88, 90, 91, 92, 94, 95, 96, 102, 106, 117, 120, 146, 147, 155, 159
Orthodox Church, 137
Orthodox religions, 147, 155
Osiris, 8, 86, 101, 148
Ottoman Empire, 98

, 27, 32, 45, 48, 51, 78, 88,
,1, 163
Pai... s, 25, 27, 61, 91, 101
Panama, 78
Park, 156
Party of Davos, 34
Passion, 63
Paul, 11, 29, 30, 33, 55, 137, 138, 162
Peace, 4, 34, 94
Peace (see also Hetep), 4, 34, 94
Pentateuch, 12
Pentecostalism, 40, 79
Pentecostals, 29, 35, 38
People for the American Way, 35, 162
perennial philosophy, 7, 8, 161
Persia, 54
Persians, 7, 54
Pharaoh, 40, 48, 51, 52, 54
Pharisees, 10, 141
Philippines, 78
philosophical research, who am I?m what is life all about? why am I here?, 111
Philosophy, 3, 103, 109, 110, 112, 126, 161, 163
physical world, 109, 142
Plato, 109, 111, 114
Politics, 4, 26, 71, 162
polytheism, 22
Pope, western, 78
pre-Christian, 7
pre-Islamic, 7
pre-Judaic, 7, 103
pressure, 101, 122, 129
priests and priestesses, 40
Primeval Waters, 145
Protestant, 26, 29, 35, 79
Protestantism, 30
Protestants, 63, 79, 162
Psyche, 103, 105
psychologist, 107
Ptah, 139
Puerto Rico, 78
Puritans, 35
Pyramids, 53
Pythagoras, 8

Pythagoreanism, 8
quantum physics, 127, 147, 149
Ra, 8, 144, 145, 157
Rabbinic Judaism, 11, 12
Racism, 60, 163
Rama, 52
Ramayana, 52, 163
Rameses II, 48
Rape, 77
Rapture, 162
Rauch, 11
Reality, 4, 109
Reconstructionism, 28, 29
Red, 29, 45, 46, 62, 129, 158
Red Sea, 45, 46, 62
Religion, 2, 3, 4, 7, 10, 48, 52, 54, 57, 65, 71, 86, 94, 96, 100, 119, 120, 126, 131, 146, 147, 151, 162, 163
Religious fundamentalism, 72
Republican Party, 26, 29, 30, 36, 37, 38, 39, 44, 68, 69, 79
Resurrection, 75
rich and powerful, 82
Rik, 53
Ritual, 96, 147, 156
Rituals, 161
Robertson, Pat, 19, 35, 39, 41
Robocop, 121
Roman, 7, 10, 12, 21, 22, 31, 35, 55, 56, 60, 65, 74, 78, 83, 95, 96, 120, 161
Roman Catholic, 12, 31, 35, 55, 63, 95, 96
Roman XE "Roman" Empire, 21, 60, 65, 83
Roman Empire, 10
Roman polytheism, 22
Romans, 10, 11, 15, 16, 21, 22, 54, 56, 65, 77
Rome, 65, 74, 95, 117, 120, 121
Rosicrucians, 31
Sadducees, 10
Saints, 39
Sanskrit, 161, 163
Satan, 9, 13, 14, 47
Saudi Arabia, 41, 60, 79
School, 161, 163

The Limits of Faith

Second Great Awakening, 79
See also Ra-Hrakti, 8, 144, 145, 157
Self (see Ba, soul, Spirit, Universal, Ba, Neter, Heru)., 15, 141, 145
Self (seeBasoulSpiritUniversal BaNeterHorus)., 145
Sema, 15
Semitic, 51, 61, 94, 162
Sept. 11, 2001, 41, 42
Septuagint, 54
Set, 10
Shah, 81
Shetaut Neter, 15
Shetaut Neter See also Egyptian Religion, 15
Shunya, 127
Signs, 93, 101
Sin, 94
slavery, 34, 54, 59, 72, 79
Society, 69
Socrates, 114
Soul, 105
South America, 71
Soviet Union, 81
Spain, 31, 74, 75, 76, 77
Spirit, 11, 15, 31, 79, 137, 141, 143
St. Augustine, 9, 53
State of Israel, 51
Sudan, 7, 77
Sunni, Islam, 79
Superpower, 43
Supreme being, 86
Supreme Being, 8, 10, 11, 14, 15, 33, 34, 72, 86, 97, 140, 141, 144
Supreme Court, 19, 69
survival of the fittest, 59, 152
Talmud, 12, 161
Tao, 104, 128, 159
Taoists, 120
Teacher, 3
Television, 143, 161
Tem, 145
Temple, 9, 10, 11, 12, 13, 17, 55
The Black, 163
The God, 41, 161
The Gods, 161

Theocracy, 37, 162
Theodosius, 60
Theology, 3, 139, 163
time and space, 114, 122, 124, 125, 126, 128, 130, 142, 150, 158, 159
Torah, 8, 12, 61, 161
Tradition, 52, 161
transcendental reality, 83, 141, 159
Transcendental Self, 15
Treaty of Tripoli, 34
Truth, 102
Turkey, 98
turn the other cheek, 19
United Nations, 28, 77, 88, 163
United States of America, 34, 38, 65, 71, 78, 87, 96, 123
Upanishads, 52, 84, 145
Ur, 51
USA, West, 57, 60, 65, 66, 88
Vaishnava, 52
Vandals, 60
Vatican, 61
Vedanta, 3, 128, 157, 163
Vedantic. See also Vedanta, 106, 108, 111
Vedas, 52, 53, 163
Vedic, 52, 157
Venezuela, 78, 162
Vietnam, 65
Vikings, 60, 76
Violence, 55
Vishnu, 52, 157
Visigoths, 74, 75, 76, 77
Wahhabism, 79
Wall Street, 162
wars, 7, 10, 19, 28, 53, 56, 58, 60, 65, 67, 72, 75, 78, 97, 155
Washington, George, 33
Water, 139
weapons of mass destruction, 59
Western civilization, 95
Western Culture, 103
western religions, 62, 63, 65
Western religions, 65, 83, 86, 130, 138, 152, 153, 154, 155, 156

Western, West, 77, 88, 111, 133, 140, 144
White, 24, 129, 158, 161, 162
Who am I, 83, 84
word of God, 20, 63
World War II, 27
Yahweh, 86
Yoga, 3, 15
Yuga, 157
Yuga (Kali, Maha, Dwarpar, Treta, Satya), 157

Zealots, 10
Zen Buddhism, 41
Zion, 88
Zionism, 26, 29, 88, 101, 106
Zionist, 27, 93, 106
Zoroaster, 86
Zoroastrian traditions, 14, 117
Zoroastrian, Zoroastrianism, 9, 11, 13, 14, 47, 117
Zoroastrianism, 10, 11, 13, 14, 21, 161

The Limits of Faith

OTHER BOOKS BY THE AUTHOR
To order check at your local bookstore or Go to
http://www.booksurge.com/author.php3?accountID=LBGT00002

or call (305) 378-6253

1. 42 Precepts of Maat
2. African Dionysus: From Egypt to Greece: The Egyptian Origins of Greek Culture and Religion
3. African Origins of Civilization Book 1 (Soft Cover)
4. African Origins of Civilization Book 2 (Soft Cover)
5. African Origins of Hatha Yoga
6. African Religion VOL 1- Anunian Theology
7. African Religion VOL 2 - Egyptian Yoga Vol 2: Theban Theology
8. African Religion VOL 3: Memphite Theology
9. African Religion VOL 4- Asarian Theology
10. African Religion VOL 5: Goddess and Egyptian Mysteries
11. Ancient Egyptian Buddha
12. Black Ancient Egyptians
13. Death of American Empire
14. Egypt and India
15. Egyptian Book of the Dead
16. Egyptian Mysteries 1
17. Egyptian Mysteries 2
18. Egyptian Mysteries 3
19. Egyptian Proverbs
20. Egyptian Tantra Yoga: Love, Sex, Marriage, and Spiritual Enlightenment
21. Egyptian Yoga Exercise Workout Book
22. Egyptian Yoga: Philosophy of Enlightenment Vol. 1
23. Glorious Light Meditation (Book)
24. God of Love -Path of Divine Love
25. Healing the Criminal Heart 1
26. Initiation Into Egyptian Yoga
27. Kemetic Diet: Food for Body, Mind, and Soul
28. Maat Philosophy (Old Name- Wisdom of Maati)
29. Meditation: The Ancient Egyptian Path to Enlightenment
30. Mysteries of Isis
31. Mystical Journey From Jesus to Christ(Note: Title Change: Old Title: Christian Yoga)
32. Parents Guide to The Ausarian Resurrection Myth
33. Poetry -The Secret Lotus
34. Self-Publishing For Profit: Inner Fulfillment and Service to Humanity
35. Story of Asar, Aset and Heru
36. Temple Ritual-Secrets of Mythic Ritual Reenactment of the Sacred Mysteries -Theater and Drama
37. The Serpent Power (New expanded Edition)
38. War of Heru and Set

www.ingramcontent.com/pod-product-compliance
Lightning Source LLC
Chambersburg PA
CBHW071452080526
44587CB00014B/2082